A Closer Walk
With God

Other Books by Jim Rosemergy

A Recent Revelation
The Watcher
Transcendence Through Humility
Living The Mystical Life Today
A Daily Guide to Spiritual Living
Even Mystics Have Bills to Pay
The Sacred Human

A Closer Walk
With God

Jim Rosemergy

AWAKENING

Acropolis Books, Publisher
Lakewood, Colorado • Austell, Georgia

Library Of Congress Cataloging-in-Publication Data

Rosemergy, Jim.
　A closer walk with God / Jim Rosemergy.
　　　p.　　cm.
　Originally published: Lee's Summit, Mo. : Inner Journey, 1991
　ISBN 1-889051-21-7 (pbk. : alk. paper)
　1. Prayer--Unity School of Christianity.　I. Title
[BV210.2.R65　1997]
248.3' 2--dc21
　　　　　　　　　　　　　　　　　　　　　　　　　97-17868
　　　　　　　　　　　　　　　　　　　　　　　　　CIP

This book is printed on acid free paper that meets the American National Standards Institute Z 39.48 Standard

Ordained by Spirit, Inner Journey's purpose is to quicken and foster humankind's natural inclination to discover the truth of being.

A Closer Walk with God is dedicated to the Silence.

Acknowledgments

My awestruck appreciation to the people I have watched give themselves to God and Truth.

TABLE OF CONTENTS

TABLE OF CONTENTS

INTRODUCTION

Because you are a reader of spiritual literature, it is obvious you desire a closer walk with God. Religious rites, attendance at spiritual services, and even late-night discussions about God with friends are all evidence that we sense our destiny is a closer walk with God. Do we not entertain the possibility we can actually know God in an intimate and personal way?

May the ensuing chapters and exercises be guideposts for this relationship. Dear friend, do not let *A Closer Walk with God* be a travelogue in which you are exposed to the wonder of the journey through someone else's experiences. The principles and practice of prayer are not simply to be read. Let them be an invitation you answer as you embark upon your own journey into the kingdom of God. Discover the purpose of prayer, and why the most ideal name for prayer is silence. Learn to utilize affirmations and denials as a lifting wind rather than as consciousness conditioners. Begin to see "The Lord's Prayer" as more than words to be uttered.

Join me in *A Closer Walk with God* and acknowledge that although we walk hand in hand, we also rest in the palm of "God's hand." Perhaps, we will call one another friend, but let us also be like Abraham and call God our Friend.

CHAPTER ONE

THE PRAYER OF THE DIVINE BEING

Prayer's Purpose

It is human need that first turns us to God. The soil lacks rain; therefore, we pray. The body is riddled with disease, so we call for God's intervention. Unpaid bills and difficult decisions turn us Godward. Whenever humankind feels impotent, it prays and beseeches the Almighty.

At times, Spirit seems to answer, but for many people prayer appears to yield no results. We feel unworthy and wonder if God has forsaken us. Many a fist have been shaken to the sky because we perceive Spirit has not given us what we want. Eventually, we realize that our supplications and affirmations have a human origin. This is why they are ineffective. The answer is to pray the prayer of those who know their divine origin—the prayer of the divine being.

Prayer is a mystery and will continue to puzzle us until it is no longer an attempt to have God serve us. Did Jesus not tell us that the kingdom of heaven was within us? Did the Master not say His kingdom was not of the earth? In spite of these statements, we persist in asking God to "come down" and repair our human world. Speculate for a moment. How many people have prayed for world peace during the last two thousand years? War and rumors of war are still prevalent, and peace is not established. If God is withholding His peace, we would think that the sheer number of our prayers would have convinced Him of our sincerity.

Our response has been to pray harder and longer and on occasion to try to be better human beings. We may even visit shrines where God's power is reported to have been expressed or go to people who are obviously close to God and ask that they intervene on our behalf. The spiritual quest in all its many forms continues, but the answer is so simple: world peace is not a reality, bodies are not healed, famine continues, limiting decisions are made because "we ask amiss." We have not yet discovered the purpose of prayer, and therefore the prayer of the divine being is outside our grasp.

Prayer's purpose is not to enlist Spirit's assistance in living a better human life. A better human life is not the issue. Instead, let us ask if we are willing to live a spiritual life. We will discover the prayer of the divine being when we no longer seek a better human life, but desire to awaken to our spiritual identity and to the beauty and vastness of God's kingdom.

Let us assume there is a special person we have always wanted to meet, talk with, and become friends with. Would this ever occur if we constantly asked her to send us money and to give us things? If she did grant one of our wishes—an extravagant gift, let us say—would we be content? Would not our deepest desire for a meaningful relationship with that person still remain our desire?

Know God
The prayer of the divine being does not ask for "stuff" or assistance in living on earth. The divine being knows

that neither God's kingdom nor Spirit's will is of the earth. The prayer of the divine being is humankind's answer to Spirit's call, KNOW ME. This is prayer's purpose—to know God, to awaken to and experience the Presence. This awareness, expressing itself through the law of mind action (thoughts held in mind produce after their kind), will manifest itself in ways that will make life on this planet a wonder.

Lift up Your Eyes

In the Scriptures, we are told to lift up our eyes to the hills from whence our help comes. This upward glance happens best and easiest when the eyes are closed. It is a reminder to lift up our purpose and to seek a relationship with God. Throughout the ages, our spiritual journey has begun in deprivation and lack. There has been famine in the land or some challenge in our human world. Most relationships with God begin this way, but we do not find God if we remain in this consciousness of lack. Our vision must be greater. We are not valley dwellers; we are of the mountains; we are from above. Our destiny is elevation. People who always look at the ground never see there are mountains to climb.

My friend, I have something to ask you. This book considers the power and wonder of prayer. It is hoped as you read the chapters and do the exercises, a prayer life will be born in you. However, before we consider different insights into prayer, let us lift up our eyes. Enter into a covenant with your God that for the period of time you read and work with this book, you will pray for only one thing—a consciousness of Spirit, to know God. Let us put aside our list of human wants. These are not our deepest desire. Our prayer life cannot have as its origin a sense of deprivation or lack. Let our times of stillness begin and end with these words, "God, I desire a closer walk with You. This is my only desire, for knowing You is enough."

Key Ideas

1. It is human need that first turns us to God.

2. Prayer is a mystery and will continue to puzzle us until it is no longer an attempt to have God serve us.

3. Human problems persist because "we ask amiss."

4. Prayer's purpose is not to enlist Spirit's assistance in living a better human life.

5. The prayer of the divine being comes from a desire to awaken to our spiritual nature.

6. The prayer of the divine being does not ask for assistance in living on earth.

7. The prayer of the divine being is humankind's answer to God's call–KNOW ME.

8. A prayer life cannot have as its origin a sense of deprivation or lack.

Chapter Summary

The prayer of the divine being is humankind's answer to God's call–KNOW ME.

Class Statement

I want to know God.

CHAPTER TWO

THE PRAYER OF THE HUMAN BEING

Prayer: An Extension of the Ego

The purpose of prayer is to know God and to experience the Presence. This prayer is a pure expression of the soul and its deepest desire. Few people have embarked upon this narrow and steep path, but it is our destiny. Perhaps today is our beginning.

Before we learn how to pray the prayer of the divine being, let us examine the prayer of the human being–the prayer most of us have prayed for many years. Its origin lies in human need rather than the omnipresence of God. Its beginning is not a desire to develop a close relationship with Spirit, but to have God solve a problem we are unable to solve. While the prayer of the divine being stresses the discovery that we are now one with God, the prayer of the human being dismisses this truth because a more pressing matter needs our attention. The body must be healed now. Employment is needed now. Our loneliness is so great there must be someone in our life today.

The words that flow from this consciousness of lack are often deeply felt by those who utter them, but they have no effect on the Almighty. My friend, the prayer of the human being is an extension of the ego. We want something, and we want it now. We may plead and beg or speak affirmations, but it is the little self which prays, and this self prays amiss.

5

Pause for a moment in your reading and determine if you have uttered the prayer of the human being. Has the subject of your prayer been a human need or earthly desire? If your answer is yes, we have the prayer of the human being in common. Nearly every person who has walked the earth has prayed this way.

Prayer: A Declaration of Two Powers

The cornerstone of many religious communities is the ancient Hebrew declaration: The Lord God is one. Today many people echo this truth by affirming: There is only one presence and one power in my life and in the universe, God the good, omnipotent. A realization of this truth changes the way we pray. If there is only God, it would be unthinkable for our prayers to declare two powers, but the unthinkable has been thought by us for many years.

We have trembled in fear, and consequently we have asked God to vanquish our enemies. Our fear affirms we believe the citizens of another nation might achieve dominion over us, so we pray for the great and powerful God of Jesus to defeat this lesser "power" which threatens our freedom. We have asked Spirit to overcome the "power" of illness in our lives, the "power" of negative thinking, of loneliness, of other people, and of the weather conditions. But in the mind of God, there is nothing to overcome.

When we live in a world of two powers, even if we think God is the greater power, we live in a world of conflict. God cannot be found in this world or this worldly consciousness, for in God there is no conflict. The prayer of the human being envisions victory in a war between good and evil, God and Satan. The prayer of the divine being invites the revelation that there is nothing to war against and nothing to overcome. There is only one presence and one power in my life and in the universe, God the good, omnipotent.

Resist Not

Our prayer life must not rise from resistance. Time and time again, the spiritual giants of Christianity have cautioned us, "Resist not evil" (Matthew 5:39 AV). How shocking it is to discover our prayers have been one of our greatest forms of resistance. These prayers are not only expressions of resistance; they deny there is only one Presence and one Power and affirm the "reality" of two powers. If there truly is only one power in our lives and that power is God, there is nothing to resist.

The prayer of the human being begins by eating of "*. . . the tree of the knowledge of good and evil*" (Genesis 2:9). In practical terms, this means we label or have knowledge of something, someone, or some event or condition as bad. Next, we try to change the person, thing, or condition. If we are unable to achieve the transformation, we try to enlist God's aid.

Resistance is an attempt to change an outer condition without the realization there is only God, without the realization inner changes must happen first. The prayer of the divine being seeks no initial outer changes. It is not an attempt to fix something. It is an invitation to Spirit to see through us and to know the truth that within every "sick" body is the perfect life of God, that Spirit dwells in every lonely soul, and that the mind of Christ is the light shining within every puzzled human being.

Let us return to the prayer of the divine being. Let us no longer eat of the tree of the knowledge of good and evil by labeling conditions, happenings, and people either good or bad. Let there be no attempt to fix the outer world, but rather let us allow ourselves to see the glory and splendor of God in all things and all people. When we do, the prayer which affirms two powers and is an extension of the ego will perish, and we will be one step nearer to a closer walk with God.

Key Ideas

1. The origin of the prayer of the human being lies in human need.

2. The prayer of the human being is an extension of the ego.

3. The prayer of the human being often declares two powers.

4. In the mind of God, there is nothing to overcome.

5. The prayer of the divine being invites the revelation that there is nothing to war against and nothing to overcome.

6. A prayer life must not rise from resistance.

7. The prayer of the divine being seeks no initial outer changes, nor is it an attempt to fix something.

Chapter Summary

When "prayer" rises out of human need, it is often an extension of our ego and a form of resistance which declares we believe a power other than God is at work in our life.

Class Statement

My prayers no longer rise out of human need.

CHAPTER THREE

TEACH US TO PRAY

Teach Us to Wait

Once we no longer use prayer as a way of trying to convince the Almighty to serve us, we are candidates for a closer walk with God. We say, "Teach us to pray," but the teacher hears us say, "Teach us to wait." Every teacher of spiritual lore knows that the practice of prayer is primarily the art of waiting.

As we embark upon this path, let it be known we do not *achieve* a closer walk with God. We can achieve many things in life, but an experience of the Presence does not come through our efforts. God cannot be scaled the way we climb a mountain. Discipline and persistence are developed in the seeker and skills are learned, but waiting is the primary skill to be mastered. It is like the rising of the sun. We may beg and beseech, burn incense, and practice rituals, but these human efforts do not make the sun rise. Basically, we must sit in the dark, face the east, and wait. This assures us we will witness the sunrise, but it does not lift the velvet canopy of the night.

Our way of life calls us to use affirmations and denials (statements which affirm what is true or deny what is not true) in pursuit of what is called affirmative prayer. Essentially, statements are formed which we would say if we believed we had received what we wanted. This kind of prayer is based upon Jesus' statement, ". . . *whatever you ask in prayer, believe that you have received it, and it will be yours"* (Mark 11:24). The prayer of the human being usually considers the "it" to be something tangible we want or at least something which is personal to us. An individual praying the prayer of the human being might say, "The right and perfect place of employment is coming to me now," or, "I live the abundant life, for my every need is met."

An extension of this practice of prayer is the idea we have a subconsciousness mind which can be conditioned. The conditioning occurs as we think or say an affirmation and/or denial over and over again. Through this activity, images and beliefs are stored in the subconscious mind. Then through the law, "Thoughts held in mind produce after their kind," these beliefs and images manifest themselves as our life experience. Most people are aware of the nature of seeds planted in the earth, but not everyone is familiar with the fact that thoughts, beliefs, and images are seeds which bear fruit in our lives.

We Have the Mind of the Christ

These ideas are truth-filled and helpful, but they are still steps along the spiritual path and therefore only partial truths. Several years ago, I was at a prayer retreat, and we were given a brief time to relax before one of the meals. I went to my room, not to meditate or pray, but to sit quietly and rest. While I was sitting on my bed, a voice still and small said within me, "Jim, you do not have to condition your subconscious mind anymore."

"Oh," I thought, "why not?"

"Because you have the mind of the Christ." This answer startled me, but it rang true, for I knew it was based on Paul's statement, *"But we have the mind of*

Christ" (I Corinthians 2:16). Obviously, it would be foolhardy to try to condition the Christ Mind. Instead, It needs to be released to do its sacred work and to be an avenue of divine ideas and God thoughts.

Typically, when we decide the subconscious mind must be conditioned, we sing, think, or speak a statement (an affirmation or denial) over and over again until it becomes a natural part of our being. However, remember Jesus cautioned us against *"vain repetition,"* and is it not true the Truth is already written upon our hearts?

Does this mean that our old friends, affirmations and denials, are no longer to be a part of our spiritual journey? Dear friend, they are destined to remain with us and become even more precious. But they are to be used in a different way which makes us more available to Spirit. Those who pray the prayer of the divine being know the "it" in Mark 11:24 to be a consciousness of God. The actual practice of affirmative prayer forms statements like, "I am one with God," or "I and the Father are one."

THE HIGH MEADOW

I believe the purpose of affirmations and denials is not solely to condition the subconsciousness mind, but to help release the wonders of the Christ mind within us. Imagine you are climbing a mountain. The summit is an experience of the presence of God. Through human effort you climb to a high meadow. It is a beautiful place. You can see things you have never seen before. You think you have arrived at your goal, but eventually you realize this is not the summit. The peak is shrouded in mist. You cannot even see the trailhead which leads to the experience you desire.

At the high meadow you must wait. No amount of human effort will take you higher. However, a woman is coming to show you the trailhead and to lead you higher. Her name is Grace. Through waiting and God's grace, you are taken into the mist, into the mystery that is the Presence.

In the analogy, we climb to the High Meadow through the use of affirmations and denials. These positive statements which affirm what is true and say "no" to lies and falsehoods lift us up in consciousness. Through their use we do not succumb to negative statements and thinking. We stand our ground and refuse to descend into the valley below and its limitations. During our climb to the High Meadow, there is no conditioning of the subconscious mind. Instead affirmations and denials are like a lifting wind taking us to a high state of human consciousness which feels good–the High Meadow. We are in a positive state of being, but we have not yet made contact with Spirit. From here we can descend into the valley of negativity, or we can wait for Grace to come and take us higher.

PUTTING ON OUR WINGS

Another image may be helpful in explaining this idea. You are like the great bird soaring near the cliff waiting for the unseen wind to carry you higher. By denying the seeming power of error and speaking the truth, you reach a point where you put on your wings and wait. Suddenly, the wind lifts you higher, and you are in the presence of God. However, before this happens you must learn to soar, to wait.

This is the most difficult part of developing a prayer life. It does not take a person long to know what is true and what is a lie, for such things are written on our hearts. We learn to say the right things quickly, and often can speak an eloquent public "prayer," but there is no experience of the Presence. The reason is, there is no waiting. A consciousness of God is not achieved through our efforts. We rise to the apex of human consciousness, put on our wings, and wait to be lifted higher.

How often have we spoken our truth, felt a little better, said "amen," and gone about our business, only to have the problem return? The reason this happened is simple: we did not wait. This is why when seekers say, "Teach us to pray," the teacher hears, "Teach us to wait."

LEARNING TO WAIT

The soul that waits walks with God. In human life, there are many skills to learn: listening and communication skills, organizational and leadership skills, and recreational skills. But the skill which invites a spiritual life is waiting. The Bible confirms this idea through a great promise. ". . . *but they who wait for the Lord shall renew their strength, they shall mount up with wings like eagles, they shall run and not be weary, they shall walk and not faint"* (Isaiah 40:31). Dear friend, if there is to be a closer walk with God, there must be waiting.

Waiting challenges the typical human being. We are people of action, and resting quietly in prayer seems too passive and unproductive. If God is a great mountain, then let us mount an expedition and scale this great height! This was the reasoning of the people who built and left unfinished the Tower of Babel. The message is clear. The ruins of the tower remind us that God is not achieved through human effort. However, we are not to be passive even though our *action* may appear passive. We can speak our affirmations and denials and ascend the spiritual path to the height of our humanity, but then we must wait. We must become like a child who cannot pass a crevasse in the earth. We must wait for our Father to come, sweep us up into His arms, and carry us to the other side.

The challenge of waiting is that the mind wanders. This is *normal* and to be expected. The waiting skills we are to learn gently bring us back to a steady focus upon Spirit, a resting in the everlasting arms. They remind us once more to give the gift of our attention to God. Our first action, once we become aware the mind is wandering, is watching. There is no attempt to refocus the mind. We simply watch. It is as if we are following someone and trying to determine where he is going.

What happens when we watch is illustrated by something which often occurs in the household. A child has asked to have a cookie, but the parent refuses because dinner is only a half an hour away. The child is assured that after supper he can have a cookie. While the meal is cooking, the parent sits in the nearby living room reading the evening newspaper. In a short time, the parent hears the ceramic lid of the cookie jar being removed, and therefore rises quietly and stands at the kitchen door smiling and watching the child stuff a cookie in his mouth while reaching into the jar for another snack. In a brief time, the child feels the "weight of the parent's gaze," and stops taking the treat from the cookie jar.

In our interior lives, we watch the thoughts drifting through the mind. Through unconditional observation, the mind will cease its meandering and come to rest just as the child ceased reaching for a cookie. It is at this point we resist the temptation to label the stray thought as good or bad. It is essential we not eat of the tree of the knowledge of good or evil. The thought is not good or bad. IT IS! Just as the child is not bad because he reaches for a cookie before supper.

A SIMPLE TRUTH

The next step taken is the expression of a simple truth which turns us Godward. If our prayer time has centered upon love, perhaps we might silently declare. "I am God's beloved." Sometimes, we will enter a time of prayer and meditation prepared to use a particular "simple truth" to re-center the mind. At another time, the truth will be a gift which emerges from within us. Regardless of whether it is premeditated or spontaneous, its purpose is to center us, so we can wait again.

The process described in this chapter may appear to be complex or to take a great deal of time, but in actual practice, it is accomplished in a few moments. Then we wait upon the Lord once more. During any period of quietness, this process is repeated many times; however, as it is with any skill, practice is the key. And we will have ample opportunities to practice the art of waiting, for the human mind is a rover.

Perhaps it would be helpful for us to use the following as a guide to a time of prayer and meditation in which we are opening ourselves to experience the presence of God as love. Let this be a prayer of the spiritual being; it has no purpose but to know God as love. Through the law of mind action, the consciousness which we experience will then manifest itself in our lives in ways that are none of our business . . . for God is in charge.

HELPFUL SUGGESTIONS

In developing a life of prayer, several simple suggestions might be helpful. First, it is best to pray at a specific time each day. Second, it is suggested that you have a prayer and meditation place. I have a chair which I have dedicated to the pursuit of truth. Whenever I am sitting in this chair, I am turned Godward. Sometimes I read or study, but usually I am in prayer when I sit in my green chair.

At your appointed time, go to your sanctuary or place of prayer. Sit comfortably and allow your mind to wander. Watch its inclination. What does the mind do? In what direction does it wander? Look around you and notice your surroundings. Look at details that bring you into the moment. Take a few deep breaths and close your eyes. Listen to the sounds around you. Do not label them as good or bad. Each sound brings you into the moment, and in each moment is God.

Turn your attention from the world and its challenges. Give the gift of your attention to God, for in God, there are no challenges. Let these words lift you to the height of your humanness and then wait.

God is Love.
The only Love there is.
Everywhere present.
Where can I flee from Love?

Father, do you love me?

"I am Love.
You are My beloved.
No matter what you have ever done . . . I love you.

No matter what you have left undone . . . I love you.
I will never condemn you."

Am I not made in Love's image and likeness?
God is love, and I am Love's creation.
I am love!
Love is my nature.

Father, reveal to me Your Presence and my nature.
Father, I wait for You . . .
Until You and I are one. Until there is only
You . . . there is only Love.

Let the waiting begin and when the mind wanders, let
this be the simple truth that brings you home again. *I am
God's beloved.* And wait again. And again. And again . . .

When you are ready, rise from your time of prayer
and meditation and be about your Father's business. Let
the consciousness which has emerged from within you
manifest itself in your life without any direction from
you.

With this exercise, you are developing the most
important skill a human being can develop—waiting—for
it is a bridge between human existence and a spiritual
life.

Key Ideas

1. The practice of prayer is primarily the art of waiting.

2. An experience of the Presence is not achieved
through human effort.

3. We have the mind of the Christ.

4. The purpose of affirmations and denials is not solely to condition the subconscious mind, but to lift us to the edge of our human consciousness.

5. The challenge of waiting is that the mind wanders. This is normal and to be expected.

6. When the mind wanders, remember these key words: Watch, It is, A simple truth.

Chapter Summary

The soul that waits walks with God.

Class Statement

I am waiting upon the Lord.

CHAPTER FOUR

A STRANGE FRUIT OF PRAYER

The Role of Forgiveness

I have been engaged in a life of prayer for many years, but only recently did I discover that whenever Jesus spoke of prayer, He also spoke of forgiveness. For instance, the following verses are a postlude to "The Lord's Prayer." *"For if you forgive men their trespasses, your heavenly Father also will forgive you; but if you do not forgive men their trespasses, neither will your Father forgive your trespasses"* (Matthew 6:14-15). On another occasion, Jesus told the disciples to pray affirmatively, *". . . whatever you ask in prayer, believe that you have received it, and it will be yours. And whenever you stand praying, forgive, if you have anything against any one; so that your Father also who is in heaven may forgive you your trespasses"* (Mark 11:24-25). Notice that after sharing insights regarding prayer, the Master stresses the need for forgiveness.

Perhaps you are practicing the principles which are being shared in *A Closer Walk With God,* but you feel you are making little progress toward actually knowing God and experiencing the Presence. It seems apparent from these verses that the reason we may fail to actually experience God is that we do not forgive. Our enmity toward even one human being is a barrier between us and our God. Our resentment and anger hide from us the Presence in which we live and move and have our

19

being. In short, there is a *sense* of separation. God is present, but our lack of forgiveness is a veil needing to be torn.

The verses above seem to indicate that our lack of forgiveness toward another causes God to not forgive us for our wrongs. In truth, God is love, and therefore there can be no anger and resentment in Spirit. The people of Jesus' day were in human consciousness. Because of this, the wisdom of the Christ Mind expressed spiritual insights in a way the people could understand. Undoubtedly, it seemed reasonable to them that resentment toward others was a barrier to a relationship with God. However, our ongoing understanding of God's nature, which is born of years of the study of Jesus' ministry, yields an additional helpful insight. Our resentment toward another person has no effect upon God, just as it may have no effect upon the person we resent, but our unforgiving consciousness does not permit us to experience God's love. The reason is quite simple: there is no resentment in Spirit.

God is not angry with us. God is love, and in love there is no fear or anger. In truth, God does not forgive, for where there is love there is no need to forgive. Forgiveness is the human solution which becomes necessary when we have not expressed our spiritual essence which is love. God does not enter into forgiveness. God is doing what God has always been doing—being Love!

Therefore, the need is for us to forgive, so we can experience the fullness of God's Presence. It is probably true to say we can practice the principles of prayer and sit quietly every day, but still not make contact with Spirit because we hold diligently to our justified thoughts and feelings of anger and resentment. Dear friend, it may be you are not enjoying the closer walk with God because of an unresolved hurt from the past. Haven't you carried the burden long enough? It is not a wall that protects you from hurt. It is a barrier that does not allow you to know your God.

A Fruit of Prayer

We hear others speak of the peace and joy of prayer. We listen to people tell us of insights and guidance received. We yearn for these things, but our experience is quite different. There is first a sense of peace, but then old, unresolved hurts begin to surface. There is no peace; there is a war. Perhaps we wonder if this is what Jesus meant when He said He did not come to bring peace, but a sword.

After an initial encounter with God—usually felt as peace—another fruit of prayer emerges. It seems there is a cleansing power of prayer which calls into our consciousness what is necessary for the next step of our spiritual growth. Just as plants are pruned for their growth, we are pruned so we can blossom. This pruning often calls for forgiveness. Spirit gently pushes us so we come up higher. All barriers to the presence of God must be removed.

The answer to this challenge of forgiveness is to enter into a consciousness of God as love—a love where there can be no resentment. But how can we experience the Presence when there is unforgiveness? Obviously, this is a mysterious activity of God or grace, but there are things we can do to help the process.

First, let there be a willingness to release the past hurts. Acknowledge through a written statement that these hurts are a barrier to your unfolding spiritual life and closer walk with God. For instance, "I am willing to release the anger and resentment of the past. I have carried these burdens long enough. The closer walk with God is more important to me than the justification of unforgiving thoughts and feelings."

Two Doors

Before taking the second step in our forgiveness process, it is helpful to understand the fallacy of the two doors. Many people believe there are two doors in our human life. Behind one door there are positive feelings of peace, love, and joy. Behind the second door there are feelings of guilt, anger, and frustration. For many people, there is a valiant attempt to keep this door closed and to open the other door. This is not possible, for there is only *one* door.

When the door is first opened, negative feelings and thoughts emerge, but if we allow ourselves to experience them, peace and joy will eventually fill our consciousness. An analogy might serve to further illustrate the dynamics of this process. A great river is polluted through an industrial accident. The water is flowing to the sea. The people in the cities downstream must experience the polluted water, but they know behind the pollution are the pure headwaters of the river which originate in the high mountains.

Being Totally Alive

Realizing there is only one door, we can call forth the negative feelings by thinking about the hurtful things of the past. This might best be done with a friend or spiritual counselor. As the feelings begin to flow, we

willingly experience them. This is called being totally
alive. If we are to be fully alive, we must not deny
ourselves the experience of being human. Only by
experiencing our humanity may we express our divinity.
Remember, it was Jesus who said, *"Truly, truly, I say to
you, unless one is born of water (human experience) and the
Spirit (our divinity), he cannot enter the kingdom of God"*
(John 3:5). This is only one of the ways in which we
allow ourselves to re-experience the past, for there are
many techniques which aid such a cleansing. The
principle, however, affirms the necessity of being fully
alive.

As we experience our humanity and "come alive," we
realize the "power" of negative feelings is in their threat,
not their expression. It is like being a child afraid of the
water who eventually discovers swimming is fun. In this
instance, feeling negative emotions is not fun, but it is
not the dreaded experience we thought it would be.

It is often helpful to make amends to the person we
are in contention with when our words will not contrib-
ute to deeper hurts. Talking to the person and taking
responsibility for our thoughts, feelings, and actions can
be amazingly healing. We take a chance in being
"blasted," but by stretching ourselves we embark upon
the closer walk with God.

Finally, we pray realizing that our prayer time will
quicken the pruning process. Perhaps this is another one
of Jesus' messages when He speaks of forgiveness.
Whenever we pray, we are going to be given the opportunity to forgive, for this barrier to the closer walk with
God will be exposed. Through the years, we have
missed many opportunities to forgive, but the true
tragedy has been we have built a barrier to God. Today,

the veil is being rent, and the closer walk with God has begun anew.

Key Ideas

1. Our enmity toward others is a barrier to a consciousness of God.

2. There is no anger or resentment in Spirit.

3. Resentment has no effect upon God.

4. After an initial encounter with God—usually felt as peace—another fruit of prayer emerges.

5. Prayer is a cleansing power.

6. There is only one door.

7. Be totally alive. We are totally alive when we experience the feelings which are within us.

8. Only by experiencing our humanity may we express our divinity.

9. The power of negative feelings is in their threat, not their expression.

Chapter Summary

Through forgiveness, we begin to dismantle a barrier to God we once built.

Class Statement

I am willing to forgive and to be forgiven.

CHAPTER FIVE

"THE LORD'S PRAYER"

Having discovered that forgiveness is a necessary part of the development of a life of prayer, we can begin again. There is no better beginning than an examination of "The Lord's Prayer." Millions of people have uttered these powerful words in every conceivable language. Miners trapped in a coal mine explosion have spontaneously prayed "The Lord's Prayer." Sunday services around the world include this prayer, for if not, the people do not consider their worship experience complete.

As transformative as "The Lord's Prayer" is, it is more than it appears to be, for prayer is more than words. Actually, the words we speak are, ideally, a manifestation of a soul in union with God. The words are evidence we have walked with God.

"The Lord's Prayer" gives us a rare glimpse of the consciousness or interior life of one who is one with Spirit. This precious gift Jesus gave to us is like the trellis which supports the growth of a climbing rosebush. "The Lord's Prayer" is the trellis upon which our spiritual life can grow and blossom. It is a blueprint founded upon Truth which outlines the structure of our interior life. The statements that make up the prayer are principles of life. Jesus can only be delighted when we say "The Lord's Prayer" again and again until it is memorized and we teach it to our youngsters in Sunday school. Yet let us also be willing to believe His hope is that our insight into prayer is more than words to be uttered. He is saying to us, "When you pray or seek to experience the closer walk with God, do so with this understanding. . . ."

Our Father

Whenever we seek to become aware of the presence of God, let us do so with the understanding there is one Creator for all human beings. God does not favor one person over another. Prayers which ask God to bless one person and not another or which plead for assistance on the battlefield are not heeded. God is the one Father of us all.

Father is a powerful word which was new to the people of Jesus' day. The people did not think of God as Father. Their God was in the mountains or living in a majestic place like Herod's temple in Jerusalem; however, the Carpenter of Nazareth brought to the people the idea of the closeness of Spirit. It is no wonder that when He began His ministry, Jesus said *". . . the kingdom of heaven is at hand"* (Matthew 4:17). This truth served as a stepping stone for humanity until it could embrace the idea God is omnipresent–everywhere equally present.

Who Art in Heaven

Whenever we seek to become aware of the presence of God, let us do so with the understanding Spirit indwells us and is, therefore, closer than hands and feet and breathing. This short declaration of truth is particularly important when united with Jesus' statement that the kingdom is within us. It is now clear if we are to enjoy a closer walk with God, we must venture within ourselves.

God is everywhere present, but the secret place of the Most High is within us. Is this not where we want our God to be? Then there is no place in the universe where we are alone or without spiritual resources to do what must be done by us.

When we embark upon the inner journey, we discover ourselves. At first, the human self is revealed to us, but eventually as we move deeper into the kingdom, we find the image of God which is the truth of being.

Hallowed Be Thy Name

Whenever we seek to become aware of the presence of God, let us do so with the understanding God's nature is holy and sacred. Please remember God is not made in our image and after our likeness. Too often, we initiate the reversibility principle and attribute a human quality, like anger, to God. God's name or nature is love, and in love there is no anger.

As far-reaching and puzzling as it may be, the truth remains—God's nature and our own essence are the same. This is a natural conclusion when we realize the implications of being made in the image of God. In addition, how powerful it is to know the holy and sacred nature of God is our essence, and therefore nothing needs to be added to us. Prayers calling for love, strength, and the various qualities of Spirit to be added unto us are fruitless. All we seek is already present as a part of our nature. All we seek, we are!

Thy Kingdom Come, Thy Will Be Done, on Earth as it Is in Heaven

Whenever we seek to become aware of the presence of God, let us do so with the understanding of how the presence of God manifests Itself in our lives. Within the simple words, *"thy kingdom come, thy will be done, on earth as it is in heaven,"* is the key to the working of the universe! God's will is done, God's kingdom comes, or is made manifest through the great law: *"on earth as it is in heaven."*

This truth has been expressed in many ways throughout the ages. Since earth is symbolic of tangible manifestation and because heaven represents a consciousness of Spirit, some write the great law: as within, so without. Jesus declared the same idea when He said, *". . . seek first his kingdom . . . and all these things shall be yours as well"* (Matthew 6:33).

When we understand this principle, we no longer ask for specific happenings or demonstrations. Nothing is going to manifest itself and remain a part of our lives until it is first a part of our interior life. Then, and only then, will it come into being on earth. A failure to understand how the universe works results in much frustration for humankind.

Often, we forget or ignore the truth that what we experience is mothered within us, not in the outer world. Ideally, the origin of our life experience is not human consciousness with all its errors and limitations, but a consciousness of God which manifests itself as harmony and order.

Give Us this Day Our Daily Bread

As I look at these words, my military background identifies them as a command. If I personalized this command, it would proclaim, "Give me this day my daily bread." Dear friend, I am uncomfortable giving God commands because prayer is not an attempt to have Spirit serve us; through prayer, we serve Spirit.

There is a key insight which unlocks the mystery of the verses which seem to be commands. I believe that part of each "command" is a silent "you." *"(You) Give us this day our daily bread."* This verse in "The Lord's Prayer" is not a command we give the Almighty. It is an acknowledgment God is our source and supply.

Most of humankind considers "daily bread" to be derived from wheat. If this were true, there would be no famine on earth, for God would supply this needed commodity to the people of Ethiopia and other deprived areas of our world. If we are to understand this part of "The Lord's Prayer," we must let go of the idea "daily bread" is of the earth. Remember, Jesus said, *". . . it is your Father's good pleasure to give you the kingdom"* (Luke 12:32). Obviously, something is being offered to us every day, and we do not know what it is. Spirit has but one "thing" to give us. The gift is God.

A consciousness of God is our "daily bread" and our unseen Supply. It will manifest itself first as feelings of well-being and security. Then, through the law of mind action, it will appear as whatever we need to meet our earthly needs and obligations.

And (You) Forgive Us Our Debts, as We Also Have Forgiven Our Debtors

This verse seems to say if we withhold love from someone, then God will withhold love from us; if we fail to forgive another, then Spirit will not forgive us. The truth is, because God is love, our Father cannot withhold love from us. Can the sun cease to shine because of the atrocities committed by human beings? The sun must be true to its nature which is to shine; so it is with God.

Every person on earth is made in the image of love, for God is love. Why, then, do we not feel this love that is the truth of our being? For the same reason those who dwell in caves do not see the light. We do not feel divine love because we dwell in the darkness of resentment and withhold love from others. Naturally, we think God has ceased loving us or chosen not to love us, but this is not true. The only love experienced by human beings is that which flows forth from within us. If love is to become real, then let it be expressed. In summary, Jesus is saying when you pray or seek to experience the closer walk with God, do so with this understanding: You cannot experience the presence of God as love while you hold ill feelings toward another person. Your feelings of unforgiveness hide from you the other person's spiritual nature and your own loving self. As long as you are angry with another individual, you will not be able to experience the love of God. So forgive, and discover you have always been God's beloved, and you always will be.

And (You) Lead Us Not into Temptation, but (You) Deliver Us from Evil

This "command" within "The Lord's Prayer" is the most puzzling for many people. A good truth student cannot imagine God leading anyone into temptation.

When the silent "You" is included in the verse, the words which have puzzled many are simplified. Jesus is saying to us when we pray or seek to experience the Presence, we should do so with the understanding God does not lead us into temptation; God delivers us from trouble. Jesus is telling us God is not the problem; God is the answer.

For thousands of years, humankind has blamed God for its problems. Whole societies were convinced Spirit sent floods, famine, and pestilence. Long ago, as part of "The Lord's Prayer," Jesus denied this human belief. In fact, He declared God is not the cause of problems, God is the answer.

As a spiritual counselor for many years, I have consistently shared the truth there is one basic answer to all our challenges—an awareness of the Presence. Only spiritual awakening delivers us from turmoil. And eventually, a consciousness of Spirit is not a means of deliverance from suffering, but a way of life consistent with our deepest longing.

Put aside the idea God causes problems. The cause of the problem is not important. Life is not rooting out erroneous beliefs. To live is to know the Truth and to realize a *consciousness* of God is the answer. Do not brush aside the realization a *consciousness* of God delivers you from suffering and lifts you into an awareness of peace and joy. Spirit is always present, but it cannot impact your life unless there is first an awakening. This is, of course, the heart of the closer walk with God.

For Thine Is the Kingdom and the Power and the Glory Forever. Amen. (AV)

Many scholars believe the final words of "The Lord's Prayer" were not spoken by Jesus, and consequently they are not part of the prayer in some translations of the Bible. It is believed a scribe added the benediction years later. If this is true, the scribe was certainly in tune with the foundation principle of Jesus' life, for the benediction declares there is only one Presence and One Power—God. The kingdom is God; the power is God; the glory is God . . . forever. Amen.

Conclusion

The most uttered prayer in the Christian world is "The Lord's Prayer." These words are considered sacred and spoken so frequently it is accurate to say it is impossible to be the only person on earth speaking "The Lord's Prayer." Whenever we declare "Our Father" or any other statement in the prayer, someone on our planet is also saying the same verse, although the sounds uttered may be different because of our varied languages.

There is great oneness in speaking "The Lord's Prayer"; however, let us remember our insight into prayer reveals it is an experience of the presence of God. "The Lord's Prayer" is precious to humankind not only because of the words, but because the words reveal to us the nature of our unity with God and one another. Jesus blessed us with His life, for it was a closer walk with God. But in a total of fifty-four words, He also gave us a rare glimpse of the truths which make possible the spiritual life He called us to live.

Key Ideas

1. "The Lord's Prayer" is more than words.

2. "The Lord's Prayer" is a rare glimpse into the consciousness or interior life of one who is one with God.

3. The key which unlocks the meaning of the verses of "The Lord's Prayer" is: whenever you pray or seek to experience the closer walk with God, do so with this understanding . . .

Chapter Summary

Through "The Lord's Prayer," we are able to catch a glimpse of the consciousness or interior life of one who is one with God.

Class Statement

I am one with the consciousness of Jesus the Christ.

Chapter Six

Answered Prayer

Too Heavenly to Be of Earthly Good?

When a human being prays, the desired answer is for something of the earth, and there are many possibilities. We want a healing, a new job, or someone with whom to share our lives. When a spiritual being prays, there is only one answer—an awareness of the presence of God.

Most of us pray with an answer already formed in mind. The lungs must be healed, or we need a certain job with a specific company, in a particular city. "Be specific," we are enjoined. If we want a new automobile, then know in advance the color of the exterior and the interior. Mental science declares vague goals get vague results.

However, the answer to prayer can be greater than anything the human mind can conceive. Therefore, teachers tell us to say, "Thank you, God, this or something better." Perhaps employment with a different company in a foreign country would be better than what we envision. Why is it that consistently the something better is of the earth? Did Jesus not say, " . . . *take no thought about your life, what you shall eat or what you shall drink, nor about your body, what you shall put on*" (KJV, Matthew 6:25)?

It seems Jesus' "take no thought" way of life and practical Christianity's application of spiritual laws and principles to the challenges of daily living are at odds with each other, but it is not so. These seemingly opposing approaches to life are the soul's attempt to achieve the balance of being in the world, but not it. Let me attempt to put these ideas in perspective by relating an experience I had while serving a ministry.

In the congregation was a young girl with Down's Syndrome. Her mother brought her to Sunday services which she seemed to enjoy. Because she was in church and because I was the one who conducted the service, she considered me to be God. She would come through the line after the service and innocently say, "Hi, God. I love you, God." Then she would hug me and kiss me again and again. (Being a minister can be a wondrous thing.) I was embarrassed by her calling me God, but I suppose in her mind it seemed logical. The amazing thing is although she considered herself to be in the presence of God, she asked for nothing. She never pulled me aside and said, "I've got this problem. You are powerful. Can you do me a favor?" Her response was always love. Her actions were the perfect prayer.

I wonder what we would do if we thought ourselves to be in the presence of God? For what would we ask? The young girl, my loving friend, asked for nothing. Instead, she expressed her divine nature; she expressed love. She confirmed for me what the still, small voice had said many years ago. Spirit's kingdom is not of the earth, and initially neither is answered prayer. The answer is not jobs, healed bodies, or soulmates. Because prayer is an experience of the Presence, answered prayer is the discovery of who we are; it is an encounter with the Presence; it is the realization there is only God.

One of the Ten Commandments declares we are to have no graven images of our God. Let us realize a thought can be just as much a graven image and just as limiting as a statue. God is formless and infinite. Can a thought or a feeling truly portray the Infinite? Can any form or image, even light, truly describe the essence of Spirit?

Silence–Total Unconsciousness

Silence is the most accurate description I know of prayer and the Presence. Silence, prayer, or an experience of God is a state of total unconsciousness in which our senses and human faculties of thought, feeling, and imagination are asleep. This is a powerful insight bringing us deeper into the kingdom of God. Most people have experienced the silence and did not realize it because the moments of total unconsciousness are, from the human perspective, so short in duration. We don't even know we were "there" until we return.

Dear friend, do not dismiss this idea, for it is a great gift which everyone must eventually receive. Too often we think of a feeling of peace or love or an insight into ourselves, the Bible, or some situation as being the experience of God's presence. It is not true. These things are the state of pure silence *manifesting* itself in our world and appearing as our lives. It is the absolute becoming relative. This is the place where Jesus' "take no thought" way of life and the application of practical Christianity meet. The manifestation we have focused upon and cherished in the past is the Holy Spirit or the activity of God in our lives. But the encounter with God is pure silence–a silence that is not the absence of sound, but the presence of God.

I believe answered prayer must be this way, for God is infinite. No thought, feeling, or image of the mind or the earth can convey the grandeur of God. At Christmas many churches have a beautiful candlelight service. During this time, light is the symbol for the Christ Spirit within us. But as wondrous as it is, it does not even approach the beauty of the Presence which is the truth of our being. The Infinite is beyond words and by its very nature must be beyond human consciousness.

It is amazing to consider that a few moments of true silence can change our lives. God can do much work in these "fleeting moments." Dear friend, as you pray, let go the need to determine the tangible answer to your prayer. The prayer of the spiritual being has only one conclusion—Silence. There is nothing better than Silence, nothing any more transformative than Spirit. Does this seem impractical? Is it too heavenly to be of earthly good? How can an encounter with the Almighty, the Creator and Sustainer of the universe, be impractical?

Let our quest for Spirit be pure, but let us also realize that through the law of consciousness, any state of mind will manifest itself as our life experience. How will this God consciousness appear in our lives? Who can predict the outcome? No one. The manifestation is none of our business, but rest assured it will take form and be beyond our wildest imaginings. This understanding is a call for letting. Letting is Spirit's way. *"Let there be light . . . let the dry land appear . . . "* (Genesis 1:3, 9). Remember, take no thought for your life.

God Is Mystery

Mystery and faith, which are said to be the heart of a spiritual life, go hand in hand. Several years ago during a time of prayer, the voice still and small shared with me the idea God is mystery. Furthermore, it stated unless mystery was a part of my life, God was not a part of my life. For so long I had tried to control my life's direction as if I knew what was best. Now I am beginning to understand life is so grand and mysterious I would be foolish to try to set its course. Undoubtedly, my course, like everyone's, is set for the stars. I do not know my way, but I do know the beginning—an encounter with Spirit.

Let us consider the grand moments in our lives. Were they planned by us? Was there not mystery and surprise? The turning points of life, the things that happen which prove transformative, were they a part of our goals and aspirations? Most people answer these questions with an unqualified, "No!"

Answered prayer is a mystery, for it is Silence, not the specifics for which we have prayed for thousands of years. It is *God* we want! Yet, not only are we divine; we are also human. There is to be a balance point from which life is lived. We *"Render therefore to Caesar the things that are Caesar's and to God the things that are God's"* (Matthew 22:21). We are in the world, but not of it. This balance point is a part of the closer walk with God.

God as Friend

When we take a walk with a friend, we take very little with us, for the friendship provides all we need at the time. In fact, it is best to leave behind anything that may cause us to not give our full attention to the friend with whom we are walking. For instance, if we took a walk and I brought a book to read while we strolled, could we develop a true friendship?

A closer walk with God requires that full attention be given to Spirit. We cannot "serve God and mammon." We cannot focus upon Spirit and the world at the same time. In previous chapters, we have explored single-mindedness or "having no other gods before us." This single eye or focus upon Spirit culminates in "waiting upon the Lord." Eventually, through our waiting and God's grace, we experience the Presence. This is the answer to prayer. From this consciousness, ideas and opportunities come which enable us not only to face and overcome the challenges of human life, but to know the joy that is full and the peace that passes understanding.

The Delicate Balance

A delicate balance is required as we maintain our focus on Spirit and remain sensitive to ideas and opportunities. Furthermore, it is easy to lose our awareness of God when we are in pain or when we look to the world for the answer to a problem. Once lost, this special consciousness is beyond our grasp until we discover the world no longer holds what we desire. As Spirit becomes the fulfillment of our desire, harmony and peace return to us.

This process and delicate balance are like climbing a mountain. Our goal is the summit, and no matter how beautiful the view, we must not lose sight of the peak. There are times when we must concentrate upon the trail, but the summit is never forgotten. In daily life, we stray from the path by thinking the answer lies in the world. I have heard people say, "I don't have any problems that a million dollars wouldn't solve." Others declare, "When I find that right person, I will be happy." Later, I am told the man or woman of their dreams has been found. Still later, a few years after the marriage, the answer to prayer is a divorce from the one who was the "right person."

Dear friend, answered prayer is first an experience of the presence of God. This consciousness then manifests itself as ideas and opportunities. Our function is to stay centered in God and still be able to recognize the ideas which fill the mind and the opportunities which come to us. Many people believe if we keep our focus on the "mount," we will stumble on the path of life. It is the ego which asks us to believe this lie.

Let us give the gift of our attention to Spirit and remain sensitive to the world. In this way, prayer becomes our beginning and foundation. It also generates the "take no thought" way of life which Jesus endorsed. We become like the lilies of the field which do not toil or spin, yet their divine beauty and nature are evident to everyone. Is it any wonder Solomon in all his glory was not arrayed like one of these?

This is a wondrous promise. Imagine a way of life in which the major effort is not to bear fruit, but to be grounded in Spirit as the lilies are grounded in the fields. Their roots reach into the earth as our single-mindedness ventures into the kingdom of heaven. Much of the animal kingdom experiences this way of life. Instinct guides the behavior of the creatures, and their needs are fulfilled. For instance, do the bison in Yellowstone National Park take thought in growing their thick winter coats which protect them from the icy blasts of winter? What road maps or charts do the birds require as they fly south for the winter? The journey may be an arduous one, but an inner wisdom directs the path of flight.

There Are No Needs in God

We are not destined to become automatons, but we are destined to allow the Christ Mind to direct our activities. If thought is taken, let it not be for what we shall eat, drink, or wear. Instead, let it be for our Father.

Fear not, dear friend, for a consciousness of God fulfills our needs without making needs the object of our existence.

The truth is an encounter of the Presence leaves us without needs. Can we have a need when we are aware of God? Is there sickness in God consciousness? Is there lack in Spirit?

Every person who has had even a brush with religion has learned the Twenty-third psalm written by David. The first verse, *"The Lord is my shepherd, I shall not want,"* reveals the state of mind of the person who is consciously one with the One. When we are in God consciousness, we have no desire and therefore, we ask for nothing. What could we possibly need if we consciously abide in God and God abides in us?

Much of humanity considers prayer to be asking God for what we want. It is not true. Prayer may begin with a desire to know God, but once we encounter the Almighty, asking ceases. Prayer is now fulfillment and contentment. It is the soul overflowing with thanksgiving.

The Revelation

The revelation of the presence of God is mysterious and at the same time practical. Doctors are amazed when "dying" patients recover and live productive lives. We are surprised when the person who could not find a job now has to choose between two outstanding career opportunities. Eddie Rickenbacker experienced the Presence while drifting in a raft at sea; a bird landed on his head and "offered itself," so the downed aircraft crew could have nourishment. The poet, James Dillet Freeman, in a time of despair after the death of a dear one, heard the words of his famous poem "I Am There."

Sometimes short and powerful affirmations or denials fill our minds impacting us in ways which transcend the words themselves. Emilie Cady, the author of *Lessons In Truth* and *How I Used Truth,* sprained her ankle and these words flowed from within, "There is only God; all else is a lie." The consciousness which generated the affirmation and denial healed her. If the words contained the power, then anyone could speak them and mighty healings would occur around the world; however, there are no worldwide healings because words do not heal. Only an awareness of Spirit can manifest the perfection of God.

Affirmations and denials are our friends on the spiritual journey. The time will come when we no longer use them to condition our subconscious mind, for we realize we have the mind of the Christ. When this happens, these companions on the journey are then used to lift us to the height of our humanity where, through grace, we experience God. From this awareness, we will meet new friends on the journey, for new affirmations and denials will spring from within.

When Charles Fillmore was ninety-four years old, this affirmation stirred his soul as he awoke in the morning. "I fairly sizzle with zeal and enthusiasm and spring forth with a mighty faith to do those things which must be done by me." Such a statement does not rise from the human intellect. Only the mind of Christ allows the wisdom of God to surface with such beauty and power. Mr. Fillmore's affirmation simply revealed the state of his soul!

In recent years, two affirmations have emerged from my prayer life. "God is enough," and "God is mystery." These two brief statements have become grist for the mill and generated hours of contemplation and meditation. These two affirmations are dear friends which I return to again and again. Such friendships never end; they deepen.

One final aspect of answered prayer: The answer is never for one person. Answered prayer is a consciousness of God which becomes Spirit's avenue into the world. Spirit now has eyes to see, ears to hear, a voice with which to speak, hands with which to touch, and a mind and heart with which to pour the blessings of the kingdom upon humankind. Answered prayer is not only for the one; it is for the many.

Key Ideas

1. The perfect prayer is an expression of our divine nature.

2. Answered prayer is an encounter with the Presence, the discovery of who we are, the realization there is only God.

3. Silence is a state of total unconsciousness in which our senses and our human faculties of thought, feeling, and imagination are asleep.

4. Silence manifests itself as the Holy Spirit or the activity of God in our lives.

5. First Silence, a consciousness of God, and then manifestation.

6. Manifestation is none of our business.

7. There are no needs in God.

8. Answered prayer is never solely for one person. It is for the many.

Chapter Summary

The answer to prayer is a consciousness of God.

Class Statement

God is the answer to my prayer.

CHAPTER SEVEN

PRACTICING THE PRESENCE

Life Is a Consciousness of God

"Life is consciousness" is a common statement made by the New Thought religious community. These three words express a fundamental truth principle: there is a direct relationship between our thoughts, attitudes, and beliefs and what happens in our life. We are not powerless pawns whose experience is determined by other people and worldly conditions. We are responsible for what happens to us, and each of us could have authored William Ernest Henley's poem "Invictus," which concludes, "I am the master of my fate; I am the captain of my soul."

"Life is consciousness" has been a powerful ally to countless thousands of people who seek to express dominion over their circumstances. This masterful approach is not the conclusion of the story on successful living, but actually a prelude to a closer walk with God.

New insights into Truth cause us to redefine life. Most will agree life is more than the things we experience. The truth is: life is not consciousness. *Experience* is consciousness, and LIFE, vibrant, dynamic LIFE as it is meant to be, is a consciousness of God.

LIFE is not what happens to us. It is not of the earth. There may be existence, but there is no LIFE, powerful and limitless, unless we are conscious of God. It is for this reason we say prayer is life, for prayer is a consciousness of God.

47

Let us remember that any state of mind manifests itself *as* our experience. Imagine the quality of our relationships when our attitudes about people are grounded in an awareness of divine love. Imagine the security we feel when a consciousness of Spirit is our supply. Imagine what our experience would be like if we were continuously aware of the Presence. These imaginings are a part of the closer walk with God, for they quicken in us a desire to *"dwell in the house of the Lord forever"* (Psalms 23:6).

Brother Lawrence

In the 17th century, there lived a Carmelite monk named Brother Lawrence who worked in the monastery kitchen. At first he detested his job, but then he decided to do his work in the hope that every act he performed would be done from an awareness of his God. He knew if he was conscious of the Presence in which he lived and moved and had his being, his every act would be sacred. The sacredness would not be because of the act itself or because of him, but because of the divine origin from which the work was performed. Brother Lawrence committed himself to wedding the contemplation of Spirit to his daily tasks. He described the result of his endeavor in these words: " . . . feeling joys so continual and so great that I can scarce contain them!"

There are precious times when we experience the presence of God. A great peace enfolds us. We are whole, safe, secure, and loved. Something so precious is not meant for a few fleeting moments. We are destined to know this preciousness every moment of every day.

Our souls will not be content with a few moments of peace and joy. We are made to be cups overflowing with living water. We are trees of life bearing fruit in every season. When we consider such things, we draw near to the purpose and heart of life. Through the practice of the Presence, we will not only seek the center of life, we will live from its midst.

The Fragrance of the Garden

We have all walked through a garden and smelled the sweet fragrance of the flowers. When the air is still, the beauty of the flowers' aromas fills the air, but a strong breeze can dissipate this unseen, pleasant beauty. The mystics have walked the garden, smelled the fragrance, and then lost the scent as a wind moved among the flowers. The experience of the Presence is like a fragrance which is diluted by the winds of human existence. This is why it is necessary to practice the Presence, thereby perpetually renewing our relationship with Spirit. This encounter can carry us through a morning, a day, and on rare occasions for several days, but no more. A closer walk with God requires continuous attention.

Consciousness Lingers

Any consciousness or state of mind will linger. When we are angry, the feelings often remain with us for hours. How often have we struck out at a family member, co-worker, or friend because we were still angry with another person? On the other hand, an encounter with Spirit can color our world for many hours. During this time, nothing disturbs the calm peace of our soul, and we are able to look beyond appearances to behold the Christ in people who, although made in God's image, have donned an effective human disguise.

Jesus obviously lived a rich life because of His relationship with the Presence and Power He called Father. It is also accurate to say Jesus renewed His conscious contact with God on a daily basis. The wind of turmoil blew in His life just as it does for us, but Jesus took time to breathe the sweet fragrance. Is it any wonder He spent so much time in the Garden of Gethsemane?

Practice the Presence

The practices we have addressed in previous chapters are important parts of developing a prayer life. Daily prayer, meditation, and learning to wait are essential to a life of prayer, but there is more. If life is a consciousness of God, then we are to be aware of Spirit while in the midst of our every day activities. Practicing the presence of God will assist us in breathing deeply the fragrance that is Spirit's sweetness.

It is not enough to be alive, really alive, occasionally. We are to be vitally, dynamically alive each moment of every day. This is an incredible way of life and the true outcome of a closer walk with God. Be sure and give your time to periods of daily prayer and meditation, but also begin the process of practicing God's presence. This way of life weds contemplation of Spirit with daily activity.

Prayer and meditation are not always sitting and reflecting. In fact, we can find ourselves in situations when we must act decisively and swiftly. There is no time to sit and wait. We must act. An example is the quick response necessary while driving down a residential street as a child unexpectedly darts from between two parked cars. In this instance, it is important we are in a consciousness of Spirit. If we are not aware of God, our actions will rise out of human awareness. We all know the fruits of such states of mind. On the other hand if an awareness of God is maintained, when an emergency comes we can rise to the occasion because we are at peace and one with God. The outcome will be beyond human imagining.

It is like a checking account. It is necessary to make a deposit before we write checks. There are times in our lives when we give little attention to God, but when a difficult time comes, we ask for help. Sometimes we have decisions to make, but we are not in tune with the Christ Mind, and therefore our choices have a human origin. We turn to our spiritual account, but because no deposits have been made, a withdrawal is not possible. Through daily prayer, meditation, and practicing the Presence, we build up a reservoir of spiritual consciousness upon which we can perpetually draw. When challenges come, God can be the origin of our words and actions. In this way, Spirit's work is done.

In the next chapter, we will consider a normal day lived by a typical human being and how this person can wed contemplation of the divine and the tasks of daily living. We become monks of the city. Most of humankind cannot withdraw to live in the mountains, but there is a high place of spiritual awareness which awaits all who are willing to practice the presence of God. This practice is destined to become the heart of the closer walk with God.

Key Ideas

1. Experience is consciousness.

2. LIFE is a consciousness of God.

3. The sacredness of work is determined by the consciousness from which the work is performed.

4. The practice of the Presence is the wedding of the contemplation of Spirit and one's daily tasks.

5. The closer walk with God requires continuous attention.

6. Consciousness lingers.

7. It is necessary to build up a daily reservoir of spiritual consciousness.

Chapter Summary

Through the practice of the Presence, we not only seek the center of life, we live from its midst.

Class Statement

I am not alone. God is with me each moment of the day and night.

CHAPTER EIGHT

MONKS OF THE CITY

Awake O Sleeper

Life is a consciousness of God, and we are destined to be alive every moment of every day. To be alive is not only to see ourselves as physical beings breathing the earth's air, but to realize it is the breath of Spirit that sustains us. Our times of stillness and reflection are steps of the closer walk with God, but most of our hours are not spent alone in prayer. We are immersed in daily activities and interactions with people.

During every age, there are individuals who give themselves to hours of prayer and meditation. Undoubtedly, the few thousands of cloistered people residing in monasteries around the world help to maintain a spiritual consciousness that blesses the world in ways unidentifiable to the general public. However, a spiritual consciousness is not the prerogative of a few, but destined to be the experience of the many. There is an ancient echo that calls monks to the deserts and to the high and sacred places, and the same voice is now calling the people of the cities, towns, and villages to awaken to the power and presence of God.

These "monks of the city" are called to maintain a consciousness of God while fully participating in everyday life. Each day a time of prayer and reflection is maintained, but a commitment is also made to let each moment be a closer walk with God. This practice of the

Presence weds daily activities to the contemplation of Spirit. For Christians, events and truths in the Bible are the foundation of this God-centered way of life.

This practice of the Presence is the most challenging thing we will ever attempt. It calls for more persistence and commitment to Spirit than anything we have ever tried. We will fail in sustaining conscious contact with God many times, but slowly the sense of the Presence will come, and we will rejoice.

It is my hope we will begin the lifelong process of knowing God to be a part of even our most insignificant task. The truth is all work is sacred if it is done in an awareness of Spirit. There is nowhere we can go and no situation we can encounter in which the power of God is not with us. May that which follows serve as a helpful guide for those who realize life is a consciousness of God and who have heard the ancient call to be "monks of the city."

In the Beginning God

When you awaken in the morning, before you rise or utter a word, ask, "*God, my dear Friend, what shall we do together today?*" After listening, read some spiritual literature for a few minutes. You will find the silent reflection and reading help focus your day.

As you begin to rise from bed, let these words enter our mind: *I live and move and have my being in Your Presence, dear Friend.* As you move, move slowly at first, sensing the strength and energy which make even the smallest movement possible. Is it not true: *I of myself can do nothing?*

The washing of your body invites the cleansing power of Spirit: *As Jesus washed the feet of the disciples, my soul is purified by the all-knowing wisdom of the Christ mind.* On another day, imagine yourself standing on the bank of the Jordan River and answer John the Baptist's call to be baptized. As you drink water, know it to be the living water Jesus spoke of at the Samaritan well. When you eat your morning meal, experience the joy the Hebrews felt as they discovered the manna in the wilderness or consider the wonder of the feeding of the five thousand. Such simple remembrances wed daily activity with contemplation.

Poets as Well as Thinkers

Perhaps you are puzzled by the personal quality of this practice. Is our God not absolute and impersonal? Yes, one of God's "faces" is impersonal, but when Spirit is revealed to us, the experience is intimately personal. Let us also remember we are not only thinkers, but poets. The mind is an avenue of Spirit and because of this we may be excited by ideas and insights. But we are also beings of passion, for Spirit is made manifest through our feeling nature.

Continuing the Day

As you dress, clothe yourself not only with fine linen, but also with the raiment of right attitudes of mind and the radiant glory of God. While proceeding to work, ponder Jesus' statement, *"My Father is working still, and I am working"* (John 5:17). If some difficult task comes before you, perhaps you will invite God's expression through these words: *I of myself can do nothing; through Christ I can do all things.* Then enter into the task with a confidence born of Spirit rather than of your own skills and resources.

As you meet people during the day, silently bless them: *I behold the Christ in you.* Some people act in kind ways, and it is easy to see them as expressions of God. Others are more of a challenge. When you meet one of these people know this truth: *I know you; you are the Christ in disguise.*

Monastic Moments

Periodically, pause for twenty to thirty seconds and silently affirm: *I am one with the One.* These brief "monastic moments" help to discipline the soul to remember its spiritual heritage and can be a refreshing pause in the midst of a busy day. There once was a little girl who played next to a small chapel. Periodically during the day, the child would cease her playing and go inside the tiny church to sit quietly. After several minutes, she would leave the sanctuary and resume her playing. Her mother, observing the child's behavior, asked why she entered the church each day. The daughter answered, "Because God might want to say something to me." A monastic moment is your entry into the chapel, and when it is combined with waiting, you will have a greater sense of mission during the day.

If you are a person who has appointments to keep or if people come to meet with you, you can know: *The people and circumstances of this day are divine appointments. There is a deeper awareness of God awaiting me because we have come together.*

When you are waiting in line or for someone, enter into the moment where there is no time: *The movement of the heavenly bodies and the march of time have no power over me. I am patient because I live in the moment.*

As you continue through the day, let thankfulness permeate all you do. Adopt a phrase like: *"Thank you,*

God," and allow it to be the beginning and the close of many of the things you do.

The practice of the Presence is "your Father's business." You see, all work is sacred when done from an awareness of God. No kind of work is more special than any other. Ministry, for instance, is not more blessed because it takes place in God's name; however, ministry, like slicing bread, may be sacred if it is done in an awareness of Spirit.

Finally, when your day nears its completion and you are resting in your bed, let this be your last conscious thought: *I now let go and rest in your everlasting arms. Dear Friend, enlighten me in my dreams.*

I am sure as you practice the presence of God, you will discover personal evidence that you and your God are one. The truth that is revealed will set you free, and with your liberation, the imprisoned splendor that is the indwelling Christ will have another voice with which to speak and another set of hands through which to work.

Key Ideas

1. There is an ancient echo calling us to be "monks of the city."

2. Our destiny is to maintain a spiritual consciousness while fully participating in daily life.

3. The practice of the Presence is the most challenging "activity" we will ever attempt.

Chapter Summary

Daily life and a spiritual life are one.

Class Statement

I remember my oneness with God each hour of the day.

CHAPTER NINE

HOW TO PRAY FOR OTHERS

Helpless No More

Each of us, at some point in our lives, has someone close to us who is experiencing a great challenge. It may be a relative who is ill or a friend who is forlorn because of a lost love. It could be our teenage daughter addicted to drugs and unable and unwilling to stop the senseless destruction of her life. The possibilities are infinite, but the process of rendering assistance is the same.

As we have suspected for thousands of years, prayer, a consciousness of God, can have a great influence upon humanity. However, each day, millions of prayers are uttered and go unanswered. The reason is that much of humanity prays amiss. We fail to realize when we pray the prayer of the spiritual being our purpose is not to repair someone's life, but to elevate our sight. This restored "vision" gives Spirit eyes through which to see and an avenue through which to express its power and presence.

God's Way

When we persist in human consciousness, we sometimes attempt to get the other person to see it our way. We share our wisdom and wonder why it is not received or appreciated. Actually, some of our attempts to help become a wedge driving us farther apart. We try to manipulate the friend or family member. These and other methods fail for numerous reasons. First, our actions do not rise from an awareness of God. Our actions and advice come from a consciousness of concern, worry, or fear. Is it a surprise our wisdom is not helpful?

Secondly, we try to "fix" the other person. No one likes a relationship with someone who sees him less than whole. Probably the person sees himself this way, and therefore he resists someone else seeing him as incomplete. The person with the problem is looking for someone to see him whole. This is the key ingredient in the helping consciousness and praying for others.

The person in need is God's creation. Conditions and behavior do not change what God has made. We must allow ourselves to be lifted in consciousness until we see nothing to fix and nothing to change or alter. From the human perspective, this is foolishness, but for those who enjoy the closer walk with God, it is God's way.

The Hem of the Garment

In Jesus' ministry, this method of helping others is demonstrated. A story recorded in three of the gospels (Matthew 9:18-26; Mark 5:21-43; Luke 8:40-56) reveals the principles of how to pray for others. Jesus was walking to a household where a young girl had died. He was going to raise the child from the dead. Apparently, there were many people walking with Him, pressing in upon Him. Suddenly, He stopped and asked, *"Who was it that touched me* (Luke 8:45)? The disciples were puzzled by the question, for many people had touched Him, but they failed to realize Jesus' question was an inquiry as to who touched His consciousness, not His clothes.

A woman with a chronic flow of blood for twelve years was the one Jesus sought. As she moved through the throng toward Him, she thought, *"If I touch even His garments, I shall be made well* (Mark 5:28). She managed to brush His clothing, but her receptivity enabled her to touch the awareness of life and wholeness Jesus was experiencing as He journeyed to raise the young girl from the dead.

Do you think the woman knew anything of the principles of spiritual healing? I doubt it. Besides, intellectual understanding is not a prerequisite for healing, for intellectual understanding heals nothing. Was Jesus thinking about the woman? I believe the answer is no. He wasn't even thinking about the young girl. If He had been thinking of the child or the woman, there would have been no healings. Jesus was thinking about God. He was in a state of spiritual consciousness. This was the hem the woman touched. Only a consciousness of God does the sacred, healing work.

Notice in the story, Jesus did not attempt to fix the woman. He was simply centered in God. This is always the work of the healer. We are not to try to heal or change other people, but to become conscious of Spirit. Through receptivity, the other person touches the "hem" of this garment or consciousness of the Presence. Please realize the "healer" is not aware of the person who is sick or in need; the healer is aware of God!

Receptivity's Role

This is our approach to praying for others. God does no maintenance and neither do we. We are lifted into the kingdom of God where there is no need, no sickness. With this method, it is not necessary for the person in need to understand the principles involved. Receptivity is the work of the person in pain.

As we become attuned to this process, we understand the great need to come apart each day to maintain and nurture our conscious contact with God. We do not know when a willing soul will call, write, or in some way "reach" and touch our current state of mind. If we are one with God, we are instruments of peace and servants of God. If we are in human consciousness, no assistance of enduring value is rendered.

Praying with or for Others?

The truth is we do not pray with or for others. Remember, in this approach to prayer, we do not attempt to change individuals. Nor do we ask God to act, for as Joel Goldsmith has said, "What God can do, God is doing." God is being our life. Through prayer we discover the truth of being. Let us maintain our conscious contact with God and rest as a "hem" extended to any receptive soul.

Our work is to rise to the High Meadow that was mentioned in an earlier chapter and to wait. Any statements we use are directed at ourselves rather than others. Our consciousness is the issue, not the state of mind, body, or affairs of the person in need. Only by making ourselves available to Spirit may God have an avenue through which to act or a "hem" to extend to the world. Therefore, we do not give mental suggestion to other people. "You" statements are not used. (You are whole and well. You are peaceful and attuned to God.)

Since we are treating ourselves, we use "I" statements. (I am whole and well. I am peaceful and attuned to God.) Please do not think this is egotistical or self serving. Certainly, we will be blessed, but the sole purpose of Jesus' approach to prayer is to give ourselves to Spirit. As long as we think of the other person as sick, sickness is a part of our consciousness. In the kingdom of God, it is not this way. There is life and wholeness. We must allow God to illumine us to this truth.

The "I" statements we use lift us to the High Meadow where we wait upon the Lord. Suddenly, through grace, we are lifted to the summit of the mountain or the kingdom of heaven where there is only God. Now God's work is evident. The human condition changes or our view of it is transformed. This is not for us to predict, for often the changes which occur are beyond the limited vision of the human mind.

Key Ideas

1. Our purpose is not to repair a person's life, but to see with the eyes of Spirit.

2. In the kingdom of God, there is nothing to change, alter, or fix.

3. We use I statements, for we are treating ourselves.

4. By maintaining conscious contact with God, the hem of the garment is perpetually extended to humanity.

Chapter Summary

We render help to others not by trying to change them, but by resting consciously in the presence of God.

Class Statement

I am a thread in the hem of the garment.

CHAPTER TEN

MANY MANSIONS

"In my Father's house are many mansions . . . " (John 14:2 KJV). Mystical writers throughout the ages have tried to tell us about the kingdom of God. Jesus, for instance, gave parable after parable trying to tell the people about the kingdom of heaven–the consciousness of God. Within this stately kingdom there are many mansions or states of mind. No book on prayer would be complete without sharing some insights into the mansions the dedicated seeker will enter on the closer walk with God.

Please consider this chapter to be a guide to the discoveries which lie ahead. Unexplored territory can never adequately be described, but it is helpful to have a sense of what lies ahead. Each state of mind is like a great mansion, a place where we dwell. Some are filled with light and joy and others are in disrepair, dark and seemingly unfriendly.

There are human states of consciousness in which we may spend time, but we have no desire to dwell therein. Our quest is to "dwell in the house of the Lord forever," but there are other mansions we inhabit before we are prepared to experience the wonder and mystery of the Presence. For instance, how often have we built a state of mind filled with fear and a sense of separation from our God and others? This mansion is a dark place filled with anger and unresolved hurts. Guilt may reside in this mansion in one of the back rooms. The door will appear to be securely locked, but from time to time feelings of guilt and despair sweep over us. In unconscious ways, we strive to punish ourselves for our misdeeds.

Another mansion "built with human hands" is marked by a sense of lack and feelings of insecurity. No one wants to live here, but many people do. The mansion is filled with old relics because while we dwell in this mansion, we horde our possessions. The fields beyond the mansion are barren. If crops grow, a drought or plague always comes which destroys the promised harvest. For instance, we find the job we have wanted, but in it we cannot find meaning or purpose.

These are two examples of earthly mansions. Most of us are familiar with them. They are not the mansions Jesus referred to when He said, *"In my Father's house are many mansions. . . ."* Our purpose is not to explore earthly mansions built by human "hands," but heavenly states of mind deep within the kingdom of God.

The Feel Good Mansions

High on a hill there are two mansions. They appear to be identical, but they are not. As we seek a better human life, we spend a great deal of time entering and leaving one of the mansions. It represents a "feel good" state of mind. When someone says something wonderful about us or encourages us, we enter this mansion. It is a beautiful place filled with feelings of self esteem and joy. When we receive a gift or have some honor bestowed upon us, we feel good and, figuratively speaking, we enter the mansion. It is possible to read a book or attend a movie or sporting event and leave with a feeling of excitement and joy. The difficulty is the good feelings and thoughts which course through us are based on outer happenings. The good feelings are genuine, but because they have an outer origin, they are fleeting and leave no indelible mark upon the soul. Nonetheless, this earthly mansion filled with good feelings is part of our journey.

Paul knew of this mansion, and he suggested that we enter into it by thought rather than waiting for something good to happen. *"Finally, brethren, whatever is true, whatever is honorable, whatever is just, whatever is pure, whatever is lovely, whatever is gracious, if there is any excellence, if there is anything worthy of praise, think about these things"* (Philippians 4:8). We are not to be tossed to and fro by outer conditions and happenings. We can take an active role in entering this mansion. We can place ourselves in constructive surroundings and choose friends who believe life is friendly and destined for joy, peace, and love. The materials we choose to read can challenge our belief systems and inspire us to dynamic living. We can follow Paul's guidance and think about things which are lovely and pure and just.

So much for this feel good mansion. Our choice to think constructively causes us to enter this state of consciousness. However, the good feelings quickly fade when our thoughts turn negative or some challenging happening crosses our path.

We enter the other feel good mansion, not because we fill the mind with positive images and ideas but because positive images, thoughts, and ideas emerge from within us. This mansion is called the Blessed State, but before we can enter this house of the Lord, we must ascend to the High Meadow.

The High Meadow
Paul never used the phrase "High Meadow," but he would instantly recognize it, for it is the state of consciousness

he entered when he thought about things lovely, pure, and just. In Chapter Three the High Meadow was explained. It is a positive state of consciousness we enter through human effort. We think positively, and our thoughts lift us up. We feel better. Some people believe when they think positively and begin to feel good they are finished; they have achieved what they are to achieve. They feel good; that is enough. Perhaps some believe this peaceful place is the kingdom of heaven, but it is not. All are destined to go higher.

Not only is the High Meadow a place to be lifted up, it is a place to wait. When we combine our positive, meditative thinking with waiting, we are candidates for the kingdom of heaven. If Jesus stood with us in the High Meadow, He would say to us as He did to the rich young man, *"You are not far from the kingdom of God"* (Mark 12:34).

The High Meadow is a wonderful mansion near the kingdom of God, but it is not the kingdom. As the seeker waits in the High Meadow, at least three additional states will be noted: the Quiet, a creative consciousness called the Blessed State, and the Silence.

The Quiet

Upon waiting, we often enter the Quiet. We are somewhat aware of ourselves and our surroundings, but there are few thoughts, feelings, or images moving within us. The faculties of thought, feeling, and imagination are "falling asleep." They can be aroused in an instant, but they are nearing a time when they fall totally asleep. This is called the Silence and will be discussed later.

There is inner healing taking place when we are in the Quiet. We are more God's and less our own. We trust. We are willing. Renewal is the watchword of this mansion. A short time in this state of consciousness and we are refreshed. We enter into our daily activities with renewed insight and energy.

There is no asking and pleading with God in the Quiet. We return again and again to willingness and letting go. The mind may wander, but we do not resist. We watch unconditionally and return to waiting arms. Have you ever seen a child who plays for a time and then crawls into her mother's arms and rests quietly? The child may play by meandering from toy to toy, but there is something about her mother's arms that is appealing, and so the little one returns and willingly rests in the everlasting arms of her mother. This is the Quiet.

Many years ago I was leading a prayer service. We were resting in silence. I was aware of myself, but the hard edge of human consciousness was fading. A young woman was sharing this prayer time. During the time of waiting, she took a single buttercup flower and placed it in my hands which were folded in my lap. Her loving act jerked me back to earthly consciousness. I jumped and so did my friend.

After the service I remembered thinking I was not aware I had drifted into the Quiet. I was conscious of myself but had lost awareness of my surroundings. This is a characteristic of the Quiet. However, as one waits longer, the edge of our consciousness begins to fade, but never entirely while we are in the Quiet.

This is one of the mansions we may enter when we combine waiting with Paul's instruction to think about positive things. We enter the High Meadow and through grace are taken higher into the Quiet. Another possible mansion which lies beyond the High Meadow is the Blessed State.

The Blessed State

When we wait in the High Meadow, we do not always enter the Quiet. In fact, there are times when the blessing of the High Meadow is all we receive. We go no higher on the "mountain." However, there is another possibility—the Blessed State. This is different from the Quiet. Remember in the Quiet, the faculties of thought, feeling, and imagination are nearly asleep. In the Blessed State, Spirit takes hold of these faculties and pours itself through them. New insights surge through us. Our feelings are like cups overflowing with love, joy, or peace. The mind may fill with images.

All of the faculties may not be engaged at once; they seldom are, but essentially Spirit uses at least one faculty to pour itself into the individual's life and upon the planet. Words may come. A poem may be written. The solution to some problem may be realized. An insight may be received into one's human or Christ nature.

While in the Blessed State, we are alive like we have never been before. Creativity is the watchword of this mansion. The manifestation may touch us alone, or it may become a blessing to the world.

A friend once told me of an experience in which Spirit took hold of her faculty of imagination. She was in prayer and meditation and must have been in the High Meadow. Then she was lifted higher and entered the Blessed State. While in this mansion, she "saw" on the other side of the world an elderly black man kneeling in prayer. They were aware of one another and their union in Spirit. The interesting thing is my friend had a prejudice toward people whose skin was black. She did not like this about herself, but she acknowledged this part of her human nature. After her experience in the Blessed State, she was healed.

The Silence

Up to this point each of the mansions which has been described represents a state of self awareness. In the Quiet, the awareness of self, although greatly diminished, remains. In the Silence, self awareness ceases. The faculties of thought, feeling, and imagination are asleep. Now there is only God. In Chapter Six this was described as a state of total unconsciousness. Perhaps you would want to reread the appropriate portion of that chapter after completing "Many Mansions."

Generally, the Silence lasts only a few moments. However, Spirit needs only a few moments with us, and we are changed forever. Contact has been made with Spirit, but it is not conscious contact. It must be this way when we are one with the One, for God is not thought, feeling, or image. A few minutes in this mansion would be a trance state.

This brush with the Infinite now manifests itself as our lives. Our values shift. Guidance comes. We may return with a sense of mission and purpose or with the insight we are being prepared for something which lies ahead.

When we first enter the Silence or the depth of the kingdom of God and then return to our earthly awareness, we are conscious of a gap in our human awareness. We may ask, "Where have I been?" But then the fruit of the Silence begins to manifest itself. The world is not as it was before. Problems don't seem so immediate. We are more accepting of the people who once "made" us angry. We are more accepting of ourselves. Obviously, we have been somewhere–the kingdom of God. We have spent a fleeting moment in the Presence, and we will never be the same.

The House of the Lord

We can see the possibilities for our lives and a life of prayer. We can sink deep into the valley, but we are of the mountains and destined to spend our time in the High Meadow, the Quiet, the Blessed State, and the Silence. Ideally, our waking, productive hours are spent in the Blessed State, for it is highly creative and bears much fruit. This is made possible as we return again and again to the High Meadow, the Quiet, and hopefully the Silence. This is what lies ahead for all of humanity . . . to dwell in the house of the Lord forever. However, let there be caution–the Dark Night. This and other challenges of the closer walk with God are the subject of the next chapter.

Key Ideas

1. In the kingdom of God there are many mansions or states of awareness.

2. We can enter a feel good state by making constructive choices as to who our friends are, what we read, and what we think.

3. By following Paul's guidance to think about that which is lovely, pure, and just, we can enter the High Meadow.

4. If we wait at the High Meadow, we can, by grace, be lifted higher and enter the Quiet, the Blessed State, or the Silence.

5. In the Quiet, the faculties of thought, feeling, and imagination are falling asleep. In this mansion, we are renewed.

6. In the Blessed State, the faculties of thought, feeling, and imagination are avenues of God's expression.

7. In the Silence, the faculties of thought, feeling, and imagination are asleep.

Chapter Summary

By thinking about what is lovely, pure, and just, we enter the High Meadow. If we add waiting to our constructive thinking, we may, by grace, be taken to the Quiet, the Blessed State, or the Silence.

Class Statement

I wait upon Spirit and open myself to its wonders.

Chapter Eleven

The Pitfalls of Prayer

A life of prayer fills our souls to overflowing with love, peace, and joy. It is the place where dreams are born and desires are met. It is the fountainhead of contentment. It is life's highest mountain; it is also its lowest valley.

There are pitfalls of prayer. At least this is the way it appears from the human perspective. We cannot expect to live a life of prayer and reap its incredible harvest and remain as we have always been. Like the larvae which must enter the darkness of the cocoon before it can flutter from flower to flower, we enter into a divine dark, so we might see.

No book on prayer would be complete unless it addressed some of the challenges encountered on the closer walk with God. These seeming pitfalls are shared not to discourage, but to encourage the seeker. When embarking upon a journey, it is best to know a little of what lies ahead. Remember, although the cocoon is dark, it is also a shelter and the place where the greatest change occurs. Just as the larvae is of the earth, so too are we of the earth when we enter the cocoon. After we emerge, we discover we have overcome the world; we are still in it, but no longer of it.

Motivation

Before the closer walk with God begins, our reason for praying must be altered. In the beginning, we pray because we feel inadequate and are unable to fulfill our needs. Perhaps God can give us what we want, so we pray. If this is our motivation, we will never truly experience the fullness of the presence of God. We will never discover the truth of being and the wonders of life.

And so our motivation, our why, must change. Different things cause us to alter our reason for praying. Some of us have a mystical experience in which we catch a glimpse of another realm. It is as if we are standing in a forest shrouded in mist. Suddenly, the fog lifts for a few moments, and we see a stately mansion in a clearing. We forget all that has concerned us. We press forward and experience the wonders of the mansion. Perhaps we feel for the first time an unconditional love, boundless joy, or peace passing understanding. We remain in the mansion for a time, but then we leave and are unable to find this place again. We may even see it through the mist from time to time, but then the fog returns.

We will never forget this happening. As the years pass, we will try to explain it away, but an indelible mark has been made on our soul. We sense that what we have seen is more important than anything we could ever achieve or obtain on earth. And so our motivation, our why, changes.

For others, there is another beginning. There is no mystical event, but a steady, almost unperceivable change in values. We are less connected to the world. Our natural curiosity and sense of wonder cause us to want to explore the infinite. We sense the possibility of Jesus' promise that if we seek the kingdom of God, all else will be added unto us. Poetically speaking, God yearns for union with us, and we experience this feeling as a yearning for God.

Maybe we have obtained many of the pleasures of life and have discovered they grant no real contentment and joy. And so we look for something more . . . for God.

No matter what quickens our desire to know God above all else, one thing is certain—there will be times when human need causes us to want to pray for things again. Look for these times, for they will come. Each is an opportunity to deepen our commitment to know God and to allow our roots to reach deeper into the kingdom of heaven. Each time we say no to the world and yes to God, we take one more step on the closer walk.

Learning to Wait

We will not spend much time on this challenge of prayer because it was addressed in Chapter Three. In the practice of prayer, waiting challenges us most. Earthly life has conditioned us to think that what we want must be achieved, but letting is God's way. As we wait the mind wanders, and we are left with feelings of inadequacy and failure. Many people have stopped praying because of this experience.

Everyone who has ever walked this path has discovered waiting is a difficult thing. Please refer to Chapter Three for ideas on how to rise above this seeming pitfall of prayer. It is acceptance that brings us through this dark time of our closer walk. We must accept ourselves. Actually, we will discover as we learn the art of waiting we naturally become more accepting. Not only will we accept ourselves and our seeming failures, but also the weaknesses of other people. To be peaceful in the face of failure is a mark of spiritual unfoldment.

Aridity

The earth is not all green forests and plentiful fields of grain. There are also deserts. They are just as much a part of the terrain of the earth as the forests, fields, seas, and mountains. On the closer walk we will encounter bountiful fields of love and vast seas of joy . . . times when we feel as though God's hand is upon us, and we are guided. We have found our God, and all is well! And then the aridity comes. Just as the seasons move through the year, so aridity cycles through our prayer life.

Suddenly, we have lost our God. We feel empty and purposeless. We do not know our way. We wonder if we will ever find our God again. We do all the things we did before, all the things that worked, but this time nothing happens. For the individual who is dedicated to knowing God, this is a dark time.

It is also a time to not only renew our trust in Spirit, but to deepen our trust. We cannot experience the kingdom of God all at once. What our souls are willing to receive we experience, but there is always more. Aridity indicates there is more soul growth before us. Perhaps we have become complacent and taken the Presence for granted. Or perhaps it is time to venture deeper into the kingdom of God. For instance, maybe we have been experiencing the Presence as love for a number of months. Suddenly, we are in the desert. There is more to experience, but we are not ready to receive.

The aridity may indicate more forgiveness is required. We have forgiven others, now it is time to forgive ourselves. We have accepted many individuals and their behavior, but now it is time to bring some of our hidden history into the light to be accepted.

It may be that the Quiet has nurtured us, but now it is time for the Silence. Do not see this desert as devoid of life. It is teeming with the Presence we have not yet known.

Several things are necessary if we are to move beyond the arid times. First let us recommit ourselves to knowing God. Secondly, we must put aside the belief that through our efforts we can experience the Presence. Thirdly, we are to persist in waiting with the understanding that just as the earth has deserts, so does it also abound with forests, fields, seas, and mountains.

Spiritual Gluttony

If there is anything that calls for aridity, it is spiritual gluttony. When we are gluttonous, we have forsaken the quest of knowing God and made the joys of knowing God our purpose in prayer. This is an insidious and subtle thing. Remember it is God, the Silence, that is our quest—the state of unconsciousness which lies beyond all thought, feeling, and image. Then this consciousness manifests itself in our lives in wondrous ways. Those who have succumbed to spiritual gluttony have made the manifestation of the Silence their new god.

In monasteries around the world, the following scene has repeated itself for thousands of years. A young novice has come to a novice master and tells the elder of the joys of prayer and meditation—the insights received, the love and joy experienced. The novice master has smiled and then advised the seeker to put these gifts aside and return once more to the purpose of knowing God. Just as a child appreciates the gifts which a parent may give from time to time, so we give thanks for the ways the Silence manifests itself in our lives. However, the child's greatest joy is the parent. This is the most wonderful gift. As people who pray the prayer of the spiritual being, we know God is our most precious gift.

Be careful of this pitfall of prayer. Many seekers have believed themselves to be upon the path because they have experienced some of the gifts of Spirit. Because our identity is shifting from the outer to the inner, our ego is less able to sidetrack us, but it still strives to have its way. In the past, our ego was blatant in its behavior. We would hear an interior voice tell us we could not do a thing or we were good for nothing, but now our human self has gone underground. What better way to derail us than to have us think we are pursuing the spiritual path when in fact, we are not.

Beware spiritual gluttony. Remember Jesus' statement, *"I have food to eat of which you do not know"* (John 4:32). This "meat" is given in the Silence. It is our daily bread.

Phenomena

Akin to spiritual gluttony is the human tendency to pursue the phenomena associated with the spiritual journey. In Revelation 10:9-10, it is written, *"Take it and eat; it will be bitter to your stomach, but sweet as honey in your mouth."* On the closer walk we will encounter things which appear to nourish us, for they are sweet in our mouth. However, they are bitter in our stomachs. The taste may tantalize us, but the stomach is where the body takes nourishment.

Many sincere people become sidetracked because they are pursuing phenomena instead of the presence of God. Seeing visions and hearing voices have captivated many a potential seeker. It is believed such occurrences are evidence of spirituality. This is not necessarily true.

Remember there is only one purpose for prayer, and it is to know God. The gifts we receive along the way are secondary. The true sign of spirituality is not phenomena, but a dedication to waiting.

It is possible for a person to have a genuine spiritual experience. This consciousness of Spirit may manifest itself as a vision or an inaudible or audible word, but then it passes as it should. If we make this experience our purpose for prayer, the ego now has a place to hang its hat. It has an invitation to renew its reign. In fact because all experiences are stored in our subconscious mind, the lower self may actually generate a similar phenomena, but it is not genuine. It will not touch us as before.

My advice to you when phenomena occurs is to give thanks and get busy knowing God again. Throughout history it is recorded the mystics experienced phenomena from time to time, but as their spiritual lives deepened the visions, voices, and related phenomena often lessened and eventually ceased.

The Silence is our daily bread, and it takes many forms. At first, because we are familiar with the world and the faculties of thought, feeling, and image, these are used by Spirit to teach and guide us. Later they are not needed. It is like Jesus said to the Samaritan woman at the well. " . . . *but whoever drinks of the water that I shall give him will never thirst; the water that I shall give him will become in him a spring of water welling up to eternal life*" (John 4:14). Once we went to the well to drink, but now we pause to allow the living water to well up within us!

Dark Night

Prayer challenges us in many ways, but nothing is more challenging than the Dark Night. It comes after many years of prayer and meditation. Some think of it as a time when things are not going well in one's human life, but it is not so. The Dark Night is not about losing our job or being divorced. The Dark Night is not a crisis in the world. It is a crisis in the soul, a crisis of faith. It asks us, "Are you willing to be totally God's? Are you willing to die, so you might live?"

The Dark Night can come upon a person quickly, but usually its onset is gradual, perhaps over the course of years. If aridity feels like weeks or months spent in the desert, the Dark Night feels like a lifetime of wandering in a void without God.

At first, the Dark Night seems cruel to the seeker. The person is now dedicated to knowing God. In fact, the individual usually is involved not only in a life of prayer, but in activity that is for God's glory. The soul has given itself to God, and now it appears as though Spirit has rejected this devotion. It is no wonder it is called a Dark Night!

Actually, the soul is being called to totally give its life to Spirit. Jesus' night in the Garden of Gethsemane symbolizes the Dark Night. During this evening He totally let go His will and allowed Himself to become His Father's responsibility. Jesus' Dark Night lasted an evening. " . . . *not as I will, but as thou wilt*" (Matthew 26:39). Ours will last longer. We will cling to the earth for a much longer period of time.

While in the Dark Night we cannot find our God. Often old negative feelings come back. We seem to regress backwards into states of human consciousness we thought were behind us. We are convinced we are lost. How unworthy we feel. Perhaps up to this point we have been proud of our spiritual growth. Now all sense of pride passes away. All the gifts of Spirit are gone, and we have nothing. This actually is a good sign, for it indicates we have come to believe nothing but Spirit can fulfill us.

Eventually, after much anguish, we decide to continue to give ourselves to Spirit even though God seems to have rejected us. This is the story of Job. He was blessed and then all the gifts passed away. He lost his possessions, his family, his health, his friends, and his God, but He made the decision to still love God. It is this commitment that eventually lifts the night.

The Dark Night dies as we experience a kind of death. We were born into this world, of water. Now we are born into the kingdom, of Spirit. We are in the world, but not of it. All things are now in their proper place. God is first. Truly, the Dark Night is a death, a crucifixion. Beyond it is the resurrection, a new life in God. Physical death is not required. In fact, the death that is the giving up of our clinging to the earth is more difficult and far reaching than the death that is the soul's leaving of the body.

Prayer Covenant

Are you still dedicated to a closer walk with God? I hope so. It is a commitment to live, to life. Perhaps you would like to write a prayer covenant that will guide you in the immediate future as you pursue a life of prayer. Below is a covenant that you are welcome to use, but it would be best if you entered the High Meadow and then wrote your own.

It is evident to me a life without God is not a life at all. Through the years, the world has called to me, and I have answered its call. At the same time, the still, small voice of Spirit was calling, and I did not even hear it. Now I do.

My commitment is to daily renew my desire to seek first the kingdom of God. I acknowledge life is a consciousness of Spirit. Because this is true, each day I give myself to God in stillness, prayer, and meditation. Willingness, trusting, letting go, accepting, and waiting are the watchwords of my life.

When the darkness comes, I remain dedicated to loving God. Only Spirit can see me through these times. Only Grace knows the way into the light. Let me be transformed.

Here I am, Lord. Clay in your hands. Waiting as clay should wait. Unable to mold myself.

Knowing only by allowing You to shape me may I be a vessel of Your Presence. Let it be done. And it is so!

Come Apart Awhile

As you begin to enact your prayer covenant, please consider the following idea. Through the years, I have spent daily time in prayer and meditation. These quiet minutes nourished my soul. Practicing the Presence has helped to wed daily activity to the contemplation of the things of Spirit. I have grown. But I have also found for me this was not enough. To my daily commitment to prayer I have also added three day periods in which I give myself to Spirit. I have come apart awhile.

I have gone to some secluded place, usually a retreat center or monastery. I have always brought my own food and stayed totally to myself. What I did not bring was also important. I brought no books, tapes, or cassettes—nothing to distract me from giving myself to Spirit. There was no radio or any contact with the outside world. I brought a pen and notebook to write down anything that seemed important.

This was my time with God. Invariably I found that although I considered myself to be tuned in, there was a greater peace awaiting me. At first the mind was looking for something to do. This was understandable, for this was its normal mode of operation. However, after a time, the mind found its resting place and gave itself to its Creator.

Take time to come apart awhile. You will find it an important step on the closer walk with God.

Key Ideas

1. Prayer brings us face to face with our humanity.

2. Prayer's purpose is to know God.

3. Waiting unlocks the treasures of prayer.

4. The desert of God deepens our commitment to know God.

5. Silence, not the joys of knowing God, is our quest.

6. Silence, not voices, visions, and phenomena, is our daily bread.

7. In the Dark Night, we die so we might live.

Chapter Summary

A life of prayer is a journey that includes valleys as well as mountain peaks.

Class Affirmation

I am willing to experience not only the joys, but also the challenges of prayer.

Chapter Twelve

The Walk That Never Ends

A God Centered Life

I have a good friend with whom I take long walks. We stroll and talk for hours, but there always comes a time when the walk ends. However, because we are friends, I know our closer walk with one another will never end. Our walks and talks have become a way of life. Prayer, a closer walk with God, eventually becomes a walk that never ends.

Such prayer is no longer practiced in order to enhance our earthly condition. It becomes our response to Jesus' promise that the meek will inherit the earth and that by seeking the kingdom, all earthly needs will be met. No longer are we trying to make God our servant, for prayer has become an expression of our willingness to serve God.

During our "closer walk with God," I have shared principles of prayer with you. To some of you, these ideas probably seemed new, but when it comes to Truth, there is nothing new under the sun. Our thinking together has taken us into a portion of the kingdom of God which has not been explored by many people. The principles are not new; in fact, they are ancient, but our reason for praying has changed, and this has created a new approach to life.

Our emphasis is now upon a closer walk with God. We no longer ask God to do things for us or to provide us with things. Our request is a loving relationship with Spirit, for our purpose in praying is now an awareness of God.

God consciousness becomes a place from which to mount a new expedition into life. The result of this emphasis is more than specific answers to specific questions and solutions to human problems. The result is LIFE—a God centered life.

We cannot engage in a prayer whose fulfillment is a closer walk with God and maintain our old way of life. We will be led along paths, up mountains, and into valleys we have never seen before. Any encounter with the Presence changes us and allows us to probe new depths of our humanity and divinity and to explore previously unknown regions of life.

The walks I have taken with my earthly friends have changed me. I have spoken; I have listened; I have learned much. I do not expect to be the same person after the walk that I was when it began. This is the way we are to view our closer walk with God.

The Simple Life

Through the years people have told me of the impact of prayer upon their lives. These people have spoken of stunning answers to questions and solutions to problems that seemed insurmountable, but answers and solutions came, and then they were no more. That which endures is life. I have rejoiced with people when the answer came, but the greater joy is to witness a person who has made Spirit the center of his or her life.

Twentieth century technology has provided us with many labor-saving devices, yet daily living seems more complex. Often both the man and woman of the household work outside the home, and sometimes their schedules leave little time for developing a powerful, wholesome relationship. We rush home and rush out again to some activity we value. As people, we are becoming more and more effective and doing more in an earthly sense than we have ever done before. We are more productive. But there can be a frantic feeling that follows a productive day. We work hard and play hard. Life is full, but it is not simple.

The closer walk with God simplifies our lives because our values change. The efficiency that occurs is not a result of doing so much that we are stretched beyond our capacities, but in doing what we are guided to do. God-directed work is sacred, and it brings a sense of fulfillment.

One of the great gifts of a life of prayer is purpose. Our primary purpose is a consciousness of God. We have learned life has meaning when we are one with Spirit. Therefore, this part of life is not neglected. From this state of mind, our earthly life takes on new meaning. We perform our previous job with a new enthusiasm, or we suddenly change our career path.

I once received a letter from a responsible individual who had a successful career with a major company. He told me he had quit his job and was in search of God. Others probably want to do the same thing but lack the conviction to move into the unknown with such seeming abandon. I do not believe for a moment the man who wrote to me will lead an aimless life. He will find his God and much more.

Entertaining the Christ

One evening Jesus was with good friends at the house of two sisters, Mary and Martha. Mary was seated by

Jesus and listening to Him speak. Martha was being a good hostess and making sure everyone's needs were met. As she did her tasks, she became resentful that her sister was not contributing to the work. *" . . . she went to him and said, 'Lord, do you not care that my sister has left me to serve alone? Tell her then to help me.' But the Lord answered her, 'Martha, Martha, you are anxious and troubled about many things; one thing is needful. Mary has chosen the good portion, a which shall not be taken away from her' "*(Luke 10:40-42).

The truth is this: if we are to entertain the Christ, we must be both Mary and Martha. We are to give our attention to the indwelling Christ in the same way that Mary gave attention to Jesus. Doing must cease as we pray and meditate, but we are also to do the earthly things that are ours to do. These must not come from our human consciousness. When God comes first, our work is imbued with Spirit. Even seemingly mundane work becomes sacred when it is performed from a peaceful awareness of Spirit.

Life Changes

When my spiritual awakening began, it was my feeling nature that opened first. I cried and cried at what I considered to be the most inopportune times. At first, I did not like what was happening to me, but the flood-gates had opened and could not be closed. However, acceptance of the feelings and continued commitment to prayer have helped me attain a greater sensitivity to people and to Spirit. I am no longer embarrassed to cry in public. If I am overwhelmed, I am overwhelmed.

Through the years, I have witnessed and heard many examples of answered prayer and miracles. Healings have taken place, friendships restored, needs met, and job opportunities realized. From the human viewpoint, these are grand happenings, but prayer yields subtle changes too. For instance, there was a man who was distraught and crying driving home from work. He had to pull over and stop. While he rested his head on the wheel, he heard an inner voice say, "Stop struggling." With the voice came peace and the realization all would be well.

On another occasion I was finishing a counseling session with a man. We sat in silent prayer for an extended period of time. The next week when the man returned for another appointment, he told me of walking out of the door of the church and having an image from his past flash before him. It was an unresolved hurt which he knew had to be healed. This insight was a gift from Spirit.

The point is Spirit can be a continuous part of our lives. In a subtle way, we can be guided and experience "small miracles" that transform us.

Several years ago I received a letter from a woman who told me she was part of a support group. During the time the people were together, they assisted one another in "getting what they wanted." It was not working well, she said, until she and others began to seek the kingdom, an awareness of God. Since that time, there has been transformation. Many positive things have happened, but nothing more meaningful than the deepening relationship with Spirit.

Dear friend, you are destined for a closer walk with God. I believe it is what you want above all else. With this closer walk come the mysteries of God, a simplified life of purpose, and the added things Jesus said would be ours if we would seek the kingdom. Not only will there be answers to questions, but a continuous stream of guidance. There will be healings, but also a greater awareness of your innate wholeness. Your needs will be met, but you will know God is your shepherd. My friend, you are a spiritual being. Let your prayers be an expression of this truth. This is the walk that never ends.

Key Ideas

1. Prayer is our response to Jesus' promise that the meek will inherit the earth and that by seeking the kingdom, all earthly needs will be met.

2. We no longer ask God to do things for us.

3. Any encounter with the Presence changes us or, actually, allows more of what we are to come to life.

4. The closer walk with God simplifies our life.

5. One of the great gifts of a life of prayer is purpose.

Chapter Summary

We are destined for the closer walk with God which never ends.

Class Statement

I now call God my friend.

A Forty Day Guide to a Life of Prayer

Introduction

There are principles of prayer, and many of them have been outlined in the twelve chapters of *A Closer Walk With God*, but essentially prayer is an experience of the Presence. It is not enough to learn about prayer and meditation. Principles must be put into practice.

The next forty days can be an important part of the development of your prayer life. Hopefully, the following exercises and ideas will help you continue your dedication to a life of prayer. This portion of the book requires much of you. The first section was written to help you understand the mystery of prayer. The second section is designed to help you experience the mystery.

Please set aside at least twenty minutes a day for the next forty days. As you participate in the exercises, you will discover they are progressive. Just as the previous chapters built upon one another, so, too, do the daily exercises and insights take you progressively deeper into the kingdom of God.

Day One

It Is Human Need That First Turns Me to God.

It is human need that first turns us to God. What are some of the reasons you have prayed? Did you, a friend, or family member have a healing need? Did you need money or a job? Perhaps you had a major decision to make or fear ruled your life. Please indicate a few of the human needs which have caused you to pray.

1.

2.

3.

As odd as it seems, a life of prayer begins with human need, for the need turns us Godward. We have struggled and tried to do it our way, but finally we realize our limitations, and therefore we seek the Almighty's help. Please note that at this point in our "prayer life," we do not want God. We want God to do something we have been unable to do. So we turn to God.

If you currently have a human need in your life, please describe it.

Day Two

Ask and it will given to you.

"Ask, and it will be given you; seek and you will find; knock, and it will be opened to you" (Mt. 7:7). This is a simple formula for success. All we have to do is ask, seek, and knock, and we receive. However, most of us doubt the validity of this promise. We have asked and sought and, in some instances, even seemed to knock the door down, but we did not receive.

Often, it is not enough to ask. We must act. Jesus spoke of seeking and knocking because they denote action. And, of course, additional questions begin to arise: where and for what do we seek? Where is the door where we are to knock?

These questions do not need to be answered today. Our work today is to admit that we have asked but not acted. This is the way it is for most of us. What have you asked for?

Day Three

I ask amiss.

The promise revealed in Matthew 7:7 is conditional. It demands something from us before we receive. Many of the promises in the Bible are this way. James 4:3 declares that often we ask amiss. This is a subtle part of our relationship with God, but one which is crucial to our spiritual unfoldment.

We must know how to ask and what to ask for. Our problem is we are too rooted in the earth. We ask for the solution to human problems and challenges, and therefore we ask amiss. We beg and beseech, and therefore we ask amiss.

Today let us admit we do not know what to ask for or even how to ask. This admission is a new beginning. Let there be no frustration or hopelessness, for this honesty is actually a step taken on our closer walk with God. How will you take this step?

Day Four

It is God's good pleasure to give me the kingdom.

"Fear not, little flock, for it is your Father's good pleasure to give you the kingdom" (Lk. 12:32). It is obvious God is offering us the kingdom and we either do not know how to receive it, or we are unable to recognize what is being offered. How would you describe the kingdom of God?

I believe the kingdom is an awareness of God. We pray amiss when we ask for anything less than this consciousness. This explains why our prayers have not been answered. First, we have not asked for God. We have asked for our problems to be solved by God. We have not sought Spirit. We have sought something for ourselves or our loved ones. We have not knocked upon the door of the kingdom.

Today is a new beginning, for we will ask for what is being offered. Three times throughout the course of this day silently affirm: *I want to receive Your kingdom. Dear Friend, today I ask for You.*

Day Five

I desire a closer walk with God.

The closer walk with God is not getting the earthly things we want, but discovering our oneness with Spirit. This is enough, for a consciousness of God provides for every human need.

Let us create a covenant that affirms our desire for a closer walk with God and the principle that an awareness of Spirit is the answer to every human challenge. Below is an example of a covenant which has been meaningful to me. Do not use it as your own, but let it serve as a guide in developing your own covenant with Spirit. Please write your covenant after mine.

My dear Friend, I desire a closer walk with You. This is the origin of all I have ever truly desired. I know You will challenge my humanity, but it will also reveal who I am. My earthly friends help me in this way. I know with You, it is the same. For years I have clamored to have my human needs met, but now I know this way of life can be put aside. Becoming aware of You will allow Your power to be expressed as my experience. I have nothing to fear. I have everything to gain.

I know the closer walk is Your pleasure. Now I know it is my pleasure, too.

COVENANT

Day Six

I seek no outer changes.

The need for outer changes used to be the reason I prayed. My world was in need of repair. My focus upon the need to fix my life and the lives of others shielded me from knowing an awareness of God reveals a world that needs no maintenance. What is the most recent thing you have tried to fix or change? Does it still need fixing? If it is now "repaired," what else needs fixing?

In your time of stillness today, even if your world seems to be falling apart, seek no outer changes. Seek the kingdom of God, and you will find it and much more.

Day Seven

There is nothing to overcome.

Many people believe God is not the only power in the universe. There are others who insist there is only one Presence and one Power—God. For those who do not believe this, the idea of one power is absurd. There is much that can have power and dominion over us.

The key to understanding this dilemma is the realization we are spiritual beings. As human beings we can allow many things to have power over us. When it rains on our planned picnic and we become upset, there is another power in our life. When someone tells a lie about us and it disturbs us even though we know it is not true, a power other than God is active in our experience. Disease and lack are other powers that limit us when we view ourselves solely as human beings.

The good news is we are spiritual beings. When this is the truth that rules our lives, there is one Power—God. The weather, lies, disease, and lack have no dominion over what we truly are. This is the revelation that sets us free. This is why today's lesson begins with these words, There is nothing to overcome. Numerous prayers are uttered to quicken God to overcome some power which we perceive is active in our lives. This kind of prayer is not grounded in Spirit. Remember our goal is to pray the prayer of the spiritual being. Perhaps it begins with these words: *Because I am a spiritual being, there is nothing to overcome.*

What "other powers" have you believed had dominion over you? List at least five. Then say, *Because I am a spiritual being, there is nothing to overcome.*

1.

2.

3.

4.

5.

Day Eight

Knowing You will help me discover what I am.

The issues I have considered important are no longer as compelling as they used to be. They distracted me from discovering what I am. From time to time, I tried to answer the philosopher's ancient call, "Know Thyself," but to no avail. I had not learned I had to know God before I could know myself. I had forgotten I was made in the image of the Almighty. Now it seems so clear . . . as I become acquainted with my Creator, I will discover what I am. Once a minute for ten minutes say to God, *By getting to know You, I discover what I am.* Each time after you speak rest quietly. Record any insights or revelations that come to you.

Day Nine

Not by might or by power . . .

We are now establishing the prayer of the spiritual being. We are not asking God to overcome powers we think are active in our life. We are spiritual beings, and nothing has dominion over us. Disease cannot alter what we are. The image of God is never sick. We ask for no outer changes because our quest is spiritual awakening. This is our purpose in prayer. However, from a human perspective, there are things which need changing, and they will change, not by might or power, but by a consciousness of Spirit.

If our world changes, but we are not more aware of what it means to be made in God's image, we have gained little. So we seek the kingdom. We invite the hand of God upon our shoulder to awaken us from our slumber. This awakening will change the world.

Spirit has devised a plan of creation that begins with spiritual realization. This new consciousness then manifests itself as our lives and in the world. For instance, when we awaken to our wholeness in God, disease is no more. When we know God as our source, all earthly needs are met.

During the course of the remaining thirty days, when something in your outer world needs changing, remember the following scripture. *"Not by might, nor by power, but by my Spirit"* (Zechariah 4:6). It is the key to the orderly and effortless transformation of the outer world.

Day Ten

I ask believing that Spirit and I are one.

Whenever you pray, pray the prayer of faith . . . as if it is done. *"Therefore I tell you, whatever you ask in prayer, believe that you have received it, and it will be yours"* (Mk. 11:24). Our words, if words are used, must declare what we want we have. Our feelings will tell us if this is so. Surely, thanksgiving and joy will abound if we have faith.

Perhaps you will recall in Chapter Three that a spiritual being considers the *it* in Mark 11:24 to be God. This is what we really want. Therefore, let today's time of prayer and reflection begin with these words: I asking believing that Spirit and I are one. Then consider what it would be like to know without a doubt that you and Spirit are one. Ponder this question, and then listen. And then watch for thanksgiving and joy.

Day Eleven

Today I am the one who watches.

Did you notice when you prayed yesterday that your mind wandered? You worked with the idea, "I ask believing that Spirit and I are one," but that was not the only thing that entered your mind. Other thoughts of a less spiritual and truthful nature darted across your mind. This is normal. It happens to everyone. I have been engaged in a life of prayer for many years, and this unruly mind still shows itself with regularity.

For today's exercise you will use the same idea as Day Ten, but when the mind wanders, simply watch the direction your mind takes. It is important you do not condemn yourself because your mind is a rover. Think of yourself as a detective following someone. The one you are shadowing is your human mind. It is important to note detectives do not condemn the one they are following. They simply follow them to see where they go. This is your mission today . . . to follow and to watch without condemnation.

In what direction did your mind move when it wandered? Did you think about the past or the future? Did you think about people, situations?

Day Twelve

It is . . .

One of the great gifts of a life of prayer is acceptance. We become more accepting of our ourselves and others. This is because one of the first things we must "achieve" is an acceptance of our wandering mind. The mind's meandering is normal, but we usually condemn it. The truth is a wandering mind is not good or bad. It is. It happens to everyone. In every workshop I have ever given on prayer and meditation, we have discussed the human mind's tendency to wander. In every workshop there have been people who have admitted they thought they were the only ones on earth to encounter this difficulty. How nice it is to know we have company.

For today's activity, rest once again with the words, *I ask believing that Spirit and I are one.* Speak the words aloud, and then wait. In a short period of time the mind will wander. Watch it as you have before. Say to yourself, *The wandering mind is not good or bad. It is.* Then gently declare once more, I ask believing that Spirit and I are one. And watch again until the mind wanders once more. As you practice this technique, notice that over a course of time you are becoming more accepting of your mind, yourself, and others.

Day Thirteen

I am learning to wait.

Have your times of prayer ever been one-sided conversations because you told God your problems and asked for a specific solution, but never took the time to allow the answer to come? I remember being in church as a child and listening to the minister give the pastoral prayer. Usually, the pastor did most of the talking, and there was little silence. But on this Sunday, there was silence, I wondered and worried if the minister had forgotten what to say.

Now I realize waiting is the chief ingredient of prayer. We must allow Spirit to illumine us. The words we speak are not to tell God our problems or to ask Spirit to change our world or overcome a seeming power. Our words are not for God. They are for us, to lift us in consciousness, so we are more receptive to spiritual realization.

Remember the High Meadow of Chapters Three and Ten. The words we speak should be truth. They are not to spur God to action, but to turn us away from the world to God. It is like climbing the mountain and coming to the High Meadow. It is a beautiful place where we can see what we have not seen before, but it is not the top of the mountain. The summit is our goal. Our quest is not a feel good state of consciousness; it is Silence.

In today's prayer time use the affirmation, *Spirit and I are one.* Speak these words aloud and wait. The mind will wander, so watch, declare it is, and then affirm once more the simple truth, *Spirit and I are one . . .* And wait. This simple process is an invitation to Spirit. It will be repeated over and over again over the course of a lifetime. One of its gifts is acceptance. Before you begin your time of prayer, please read Isaiah 40:31.

Day Fourteen

I forgive others so I might experience God.

When we justify our anger and resentment, we cannot pray. *"So if you are offering your gift at the altar, and there remember that your brother has something against you, leave your gift there before the altar and go; first be reconciled to your brother, and then come and offer your gift"* (Mt. 5:23-24). *"And whenever you stand praying, forgive, if you have anything against any one . . . "* (Mk 11:25).

One of the reasons we have difficulty developing a relationship with God is we have strained relationships with others. Our unforgiveness is a barrier to our experience of the love God is. This is why we can be dedicated to a life of prayer and make little progress. Now is the time to leave our gift at the altar and be reconciled to our brother.

It is best if we can talk with the person that challenges us, but this is not always possible. Sometimes the person has passed on, and on other occasions it is not appropriate we make contact with the person again. However, whenever possible face to face contact is best.

If you are able to do this, please do not talk about the other person's behavior or actions. Forgiveness is a process that leaves our soul free of anger and resentment. On the surface another person's actions seem to be the root of the problem, but this is not totally true. Our beliefs and conclusions are the culprit, for they are a shield to divine love.

Talk about your own feelings and actions and admit your contribution to the problem. Expect nothing from the other person. The healing that is to occur is destined to happen in your soul, not that of the other individual. However, you will discover that often the harmony that unfolds for both of you is nothing less than divine.

If there is someone or if there are a number of people you can talk to, let forgiveness begin. Write the names of the people you will try to see.

If you are unable to literally sit and talk with your "adversary," you can experience this process through the use of your imagination. In your mind's eye, rest in a peaceful place with the other person and say the things which need to be said. If you do this, record the essence of the experience in the space provided.

Day Fifteen

I forgive myself, so I might experience God.

Often our barrier to God is our lack of forgiveness of ourselves. We have committed some wrong or some wrong has been done to us that has caused us to lose sight of our true identity. We may feel less than other people. This can be one of the most challenging things we are called to do on the spiritual path. Thank God forgiveness of ourselves is God's work, not ours!

There are steps for us to take, but the final step is taken by God as we experience the power of divine love. Our work is threefold. First, we admit to a trusted individual our wrong doings or the wrong done to us. Secondly, we share with our confidant our willingness to experience the love God is. Lastly, we give ourselves to Spirit in prayer. Follow the prayer process of Days Ten through Thirteen using the words, *I am God's beloved now and forevermore.* Return to this day after the process is complete and describe the good that has unfolded in your interior life.

Day Sixteen

Where there is love, there is no need for forgiveness.

There are usually people we need to forgive, but we are unable to speak with them. Day Fourteen suggested a simple technique for forgiveness when we are unable to talk with the other person. Today's lesson shares other techniques to help achieve the same end.

First it is important to acknowledge the need for forgiveness. The healing begins when you tell a trusted friend about your need to be reconciled with another person. It is also helpful to reveal the circumstances surrounding the feelings which have brought unrest to your life for days, weeks, or years. Just talking or thinking about the circumstances can re-ignite the emotions which you have tried to keep inside. (But you never do. In fact, the feelings come out and taint your current relationships with others as well as God.)

The feelings do not surface to make you miserable, but to be released. The forgiveness process continues when you refuse to label the feelings as good or bad. Emotions are neither good nor bad. They *are*. In other words, you are accepting a part of your interior world. You might as well accept it; it is there.

I have often suggested to an individual that he write a letter of anger to the person who has "done you wrong." Then allow the letter to rest for three days. Finally reread it, and burn it.

The first step in forgiveness is essentially getting in touch with the emotions of the past and accepting them. However, no one can remain quagmired in past hurts and find God. It is necessary to come up higher. For this important step in forgiveness, I have three suggestions. First, send an anonymous gift to the person. This can be a flower or card. In this way, you are beginning to express a positive side of your being. And it is paramount the gift be anonymous. The person must not know it is from you. The law states every gift is returned in like kind. Since the gift is anonymous, Spirit will fulfill the law. This occurs as you become more aware of God. In this instance, your gift was one of love, so love is awakened in you.

Another possibility might be to think about someone you love and allow the good feelings to emerge from within you. Form an image in your mind of the person you have good feelings about. Then allow the face of the person who challenges you to come to mind. See how long it takes before the good feelings dissipate. At first, it may be instantly, but after a time, you may see the person in a different way.

And last but not least is prayer. You can do all these things while giving yourself to love. Your willingness to sit in prayer each day and ask to experience the Presence as love will lift you up. One day, you will experience love, and then there will be no need for forgiveness.

The ideas which have been shared with you are not just for today. It may takes weeks for you to work your way through these ideas. Don't quit.

Day Seventeen

Today I call forth the cleansing power of Spirit.

Prayer is a cleansing power; that which is not like God has no place in our lives. Just as the master craftsman chips away the stone to reveal the masterpiece, so Spirit reveals and then dissolves that which is not like itself. This happens, however, only with our consent.

Our initial role is to be willing to release the past hurts and beliefs which stand between us and a closer walk with God. Write a statement of your willingness.

Our willingness combined with our prayerful invitation to the cleansing power of Spirit will cause memories and feelings to rise from within us. This is a good sign. The emotions may be hurtful, but they have not come to inflict pain. They come to be accepted and released. As you pray become sensitive to any images or feelings from the past which are painful. As they arise in the coming days and weeks, write a brief description.

There is also another possibility. Many years ago, while in prayer I was cried out of one eye. I did not know what this was about, but eventually an answer came that seemed reasonable. Crying from one eye is a sign of cleansing occurring at a deep unconscious level. Thank God we do not have to become aware again of every hurtful emotion or situation. Through the activity of the Holy Spirit, the soul is being cleansed. If this occurs in your life, give thanks.

Day Eighteen

The mark of Cain is upon me.

Remember the story of Cain and Abel. Cain killed his brother Abel and feared for his life, but God put a mark on Cain which preserved him. Have you ever wondered what the mark of Cain meant to those who saw it? Was it a mark of shame or guilt? Did it say to the one who saw it, "This man killed his brother, stay away from him"?

There are numerous possibilities, but the one that came to me years ago was that God was saying to all the world, "This one is precious to me." If God did not value Cain, why didn't God allow him to die at the hand of another? In this story, this was not permitted. I speculate this was because Cain was precious to God. The truth is we are all precious to God. The mark of Cain is upon each of us.

We are all sacred humans. I love the concept of the sacred human. I have seen the sacred one many times. I see him in the mirror in the morning, for I am a sacred human. I have seen him and her in counseling sessions when someone is hurt or upset, crying or angry. Dear friend, our humanity is to be accepted, not shunned. Think of it as a little child who is hurt. Would you shun such a little one? I doubt it. You would sweep the child into your arms and try to sooth the hurt. You would tell the little one it is going to be okay. Why will you do this with a child, but not with yourself? You try to put aside the hurt. This path does not lead to the kingdom of God.

As we bring our humanity into the light and accept it and its frailties, we will naturally find our divinity beginning to shine. The image of God finds an avenue of expression when we accept ourselves as we are. Oddly enough, we are then better able to accept others.

Let there form in your mind an image of yourself as a child. Pick a time when you were physically or emotionally hurt. As an adult, approach your younger self and accept the child. Do not put aside this part of your being. Hold the child. Tell it everything is going to be alright. Let the little one and you become one. Let the healing of the sacred human begin.

Day Nineteen

I never pray alone.

You never pray alone. There is always someone on our planet who is praying in his or her own way at the exact time you are praying. This can be a powerful awareness. This point was stressed in Chapter Five entitled, "The Lord's Prayer." As I write to you, I am making a commitment that each day of my life I will enter into the consciousness of "The Lord's Prayer." Then if you are ever feeling alone, you will know if you pray "The Lord's Prayer," someone is praying with you. Perhaps all the readers of this book could make this commitment. How great would be the united consciousness of each of us and the people around the world. If this is a commitment you can make, please sign the statement below.

I commit myself to enter into the consciousness of "The Lord's Prayer" each day, knowing that as I do, I am not alone.

_____

Signature

Day Twenty

On earth as it is in heaven . . .

Through the years, "The Lord's Prayer" has touched me in many ways. At one time or another, all the verses have become grist for the mill and the central focus of times of prayer and meditation. For the next couple of days, I want to share with you some of the implications of several of the verses.

"On earth as it is in heaven." This verse reveals the way the universe works. In Chapter Five this idea was expanded upon, but now it is time to narrow the focus of the idea to our own lives. The implications are immense. Nothing comes into being in our life that is not first born in consciousness.

Consider what is now "on earth" you wish was not a part of your life. Are you willing to entertain a new heaven, so there can be a new earth? This is the key question which the verse asks us. What would you like to come into being that currently is not part of your world?

Based on your current understanding of the way the universe works, what steps are you going to take which will bring about a new heaven and new earth in your life? Please list the steps below.

Day Twenty-One

You lead me not into temptation.

Has God ever led you into temptation? My answer is, "God never had to lead me into temptation. I could find it on my own." When we believe God is the cause of our problems, we experience helplessness. If God is against us, who can be for us? The truth is God is for us, and God does not lead us into temptation. We can find temptation all by ourselves. However, God delivers us from evil . . . from temptation and our human problems. This is a key realization.

The question is, are you willing to consider God is the answer? Please realize, God is not going to pull strings and solve your problem. In fact, unless you become aware of Spirit, nothing constructive is going to occur. In the purest sense, God is not the answer . . . *a consciousness of God is the answer.* How this awareness will manifest itself is none of your business, but it will come into being in ways that either lift you up above the problem or move you through it with swiftness.

When you firmly believe that God is not the problem, and that a consciousness of God is the answer, what will you do? How will this conviction and belief become evident?

Day Twenty-Two

I ask for only one "thing."

When we are consciously one with God, asking ceases. When we have God, what else do we need? The Bible is filled with references about asking. We can interpret the asking to be for things of the earth, but spiritual awareness reveals it is God we want. The asking opens our souls so the indwelling Lord may make itself known. And when it does, asking ceases.

A child knows this process. Let us assume a child is accompanying her mother to the grocery store, and she spies some candy she wants. The asking begins. In fact, it may become hounding or even a temper tantrum if the parent says no, but once the child has the candy in her hand, the asking ceases. When we are consciously one with God, all asking ends. Rejoicing and thanksgiving begin.

In your time of prayer and meditation today ask only for God. The "sign" you have received will be joy and thankfulness and the realization you are fulfilled and no longer need to ask.

Day Twenty-Three

When I am consciously one with God, I know what to do.

Our quest is a closer walk with God, but it is reasonable to believe life's challenges will be met when we are consciously one with Spirit. One of our challenges is knowing what to do. The choices we make impact our lives and are far reaching in their effect. Perhaps this is why we are so cautious about the choices we make. In fact, there are times we do not act when we need to because we are afraid of making the wrong choice. Most of us can point to past decisions which resulted in chaos.

When we are consciously one with God, we know what to do. The truth is we have only one choice to make: either we turn Godward or we turn to the outer world of opinions. If we turn to the world, chaos can come into being. When we turn Godward and make contact with Spirit, a divine plan unfolds.

When we pray the prayer of the spiritual being, we do not ask what to do. Remember a relationship with God is the heart of our way of life. Instead, we are willing to become consciously one with the mind of God. This oneness allows decisions to be made easily. The issue becomes not a decision to make, but whether God's wisdom will be expressed.

Remember this important insight, for there will be a time when you will want to know what to do. When this occurs, follow this process:

1. Remember, you have only one true decision to make—either you turn to God or to the world.

2. Remember the decision to be made is not the real issue. The issue is whether you will allow the wisdom of God to be expressed.

3. Rest in prayer and meditation, and give your attention to the following ideas.

> *I have the mind of the Christ.*
> *There is no indecision in me.*
> *The light of God is shining from within me.*
> *Thank you, Divine Light and Wisdom.*

4. Know that the consciousness of God experienced will manifest itself as wise decisions. Not only will the choice be made, but a foundation will have been laid to help you make wise choices in the future.

Day Twenty-Four

When I am consciously one with God, I know I am whole.

More prayer requests are made for physical healing than for any other human challenge. We want our bodies restored, but this need is not the real issue. The issue is whether we will allow Spirit to reveal our innate wholeness. True wholeness is not a function of the body. Wholeness transcends the condition of our body, for it is a part of our spiritual identity.

Jesus knew the disease and illness of the people, but He did not try to heal them. Instead He turned His attention Godward and allowed His Father to reveal to Him the spiritual nature of the people. He knew the truth about them. As spiritual beings they breathed no air and ate no food. They were pure Spirit and had never been sick. This consciousness or awareness of life was the healing agent.

Today or whenever you have a healing need, remember the following ideas:

1. Remember, the state of the physical body is not the real issue.

2. Regardless of the condition of the body, you are whole.

3. Know that only God can reveal the truth of being and your spiritual wholeness. There is no image of the mind or earth that can describe who and what you truly are.

4. This spiritual consciousness is the healing agent. The call is to give yourself to the Silence. Rest in prayer and meditation, and give your attention to the following ideas.

> *I am not the body. I am not cells and organs and tissue.*
> *I am a pure expression of divine life.*
> *The condition of the body does not change what I am.*
> *I have never been sick. Illness is not my nature.*
> *I am whole, complete, and perfect now.*

5. Remember, a consciousness of God is the healer.

Day Twenty-Five

When I am consciously one with God, I have no needs.

Making ends meet is a human challenge. Security underlies our need for money. We are told education leads to a good job, and a good job provides for our earthly needs. We are safe and secure when we are employed.

This is not true. A good job and money are not the real issue. We must find security not in the world, but in a consciousness of God. When we are consciously one with God, we have no needs. There is no need to ask for anything. We are fulfilled and content. Only an awareness of Spirit can give this gift. Employment and money cannot provide this life of peace and joy. This is God's work.

However, a consciousness of God manifests itself in mysterious ways. Maybe a prospering idea enters our mind or an opportunity comes to us that has possibilities. Because of our conscious oneness with Spirit, our earthly needs are provided for, but we also have purpose and contentment. First there is God, and then all else follows.

Today and whenever you have a prosperity need or are not feeling secure and content, ponder the following ideas.

1. Remember, money and employment are not the real issue.

2. Open yourself to a state of consciousness in which you have no needs. There will be no asking, only thanksgiving, joy, and contentment.

3. Know that only a consciousness of God can provide this heavenly state of security.

4. Rest in prayer and meditation, and give your attention to the following ideas.

> *I am secure and content, not because of the*
> *earthly things I have, but because I am*
> *consciously one with God.*
> *The pearl of great price is an awareness of Spirit.*
> *This is the coin of the realm. With it all is well.*
> *Without it life is a struggle.*
> *I am content and fulfilled.*
> *I ask for nothing, for God and I are one.*

5. Remember, in a consciousness of God, there are no needs.

Day Twenty-Six

When I am consciously one with God, I have nothing to fear.

Fear causes us to seek protection instead of God. It paralyzes us and limits our ability to function. Seemingly it is a barrier to a greater good. However, the brave achieve this good. They stand on the bridge with the coward, but the courageous move forward and as they do more of their spirituality is made manifest.

Having a purpose dissipates fear. We are no longer concerned about ourselves. There is something which must be done, and we move forward to do it.

When we know our spiritual identity, we have no fear. Protection is not the real issue. The issue is whether we will awaken to who and what we are. What can harm God's creation?

Today and whenever you experience fear, use the following ideas.

1. Remember, there is no fear in God.

2. A spiritual being aware of its identity has nothing to fear.

3. Know that only a consciousness of God can reveal this heavenly vision.

4. Rest in prayer and meditation, and give your attention to the following ideas.

There is no fear in God, and I am in God.
There is no need for protection, for I am

consciously one with God.
Who I am has never been harmed.
God is the power in my life, not fear.
I stand on the bridge willing to move forward to
do those things which ought to be done by me.

5. Remember in a consciousness of God, there is no fear.

Day Twenty-Seven

When I am consciously one with God, I know peace and joy.

Many people believe peace and joy come when conditions are what they want them to be. Peace comes when the doctor tells us the tumor is benign. We are joyful when we are picked for the new assignment. For too long peace and joy have originated in earthly conditions. When this happens, peace and joy are fleeting. We want them to be constant companions, but they are like fickle friends. They come, and they go.

There is a peace that passes understanding and a joy that is boundless. People throughout all the ages have experienced peace and joy transcending earthly conditions. In fact, in stressful conditions peace has come as a forerunner of greater good. Joy has been experienced while sitting alone late at night.

The truth is the world has no peace or joy for us. When we are consciously one with God, there is peace and joy. When we lose our sense of oneness, then peace and joy are gone. At least this is the way it seems, but the truth is peace and joy are innate to us. They are part of our spiritual nature. When we are consciously one with Spirit, what is innate to us can be experienced.

Perhaps this is a trying time for you, or perhaps you are "having a good day." Let's put to the test this ideal of oneness with God yielding peace and joy.

1. Remember, there is no true peace or joy in the world.

2. Peace and joy are found in God.

3. Know that only a consciousness of God can grant you peace and joy that pass understanding.

4. Rest in prayer and meditation, and give your attention to the following ideas.

> *I do not look to the world for peace and joy.*
> *The world cannot give me these gifts.*
> *These two are gifts of God.*
> *I turn to God in search of peace.*
> *I turn to God in search of joy.*
> *And I am blessed.*

5. Remember to return to this process whenever you have lost your sense of peace and joy or when you tend to believe the world can give you these qualities of Spirit.

Day Twenty-Eight

When I am consciously one with God, I know love.

The world makes promises it cannot keep. We have spent a lifetime being told people are the source of love. "Make people love you, and all will be well. You are empty of love, an empty vessel, waiting to be filled. Take yourself to the fountain of love called another, and allow yourself to be filled." How true these words seem. How erroneous they are.

The truth is our nature is love. God is love, and we are made in the image and after the likeness of love. We are not devoid of love. When we hug a stuffed animal we often feel loved. Why is this? Is it because the stuffed animal gives us love? No, it is because as we express love we experience it.

Today we do not look to others for what we have already been given. Love is here, and it is closer than hands and feet and breathing. Practice today's exercise, but let it also be a tool to use whenever you feel resentment or that you are not loved.

1. Remember, the source of love is not another person.

2. Love is a gift of God. It is a revelation of your true self.

3. Only by expressing your true nature may you truly experience love.

4. Rest in prayer and meditation, and give your attention to the following ideas.

Anger and resentment are not a part of my true nature.
These human emotions do not exist in God.
I am a being of Spirit.
Anger and resentment are not part of me,
for love is my nature.
I am willing to express my real self.
My loving self.
As the river of love flows from me into the sea of humanity,
I experience love.

5. Remember in a consciousness of God, there is no hurt, resentment, or sense of rejection.

Day Twenty-Nine

Manifestation is none of my business.

The things of the world have seemed incredibly important to us. What happened to us and in our world seemed paramount. Now this way of life is changing. The interior world is becoming the focus of our attention. One principle underlies this way of life. *A consciousness of God will manifest itself in wondrous and unexpected ways.* It is for this reason I say, "Manifestation is none of my business. My business is a consciousness of God."

From this awareness of Spirit, our life will flow. We do not need to be concerned with what happens to us. Only good ultimately comes from contact with God. This is an important idea. It is a cornerstone of the spiritual life.

Seven times throughout this day say to yourself, *Manifestation is none of my business.*

Before this day ends, please reread Chapters Seven and Eight in preparation for tomorrow's activities. After reading these chapters glance ahead at Day Thirty before you go to bed tonight. In this way you will be able to prepare yourself mentally and spiritually for tomorrow.

Day Thirty

God is a part of everything I do.

Imagine a day of oneness with Spirit, our attention continuously given to God. We give the gift of our attention to Spirit, and Spirit slowly reveals itself to us. This is our quest today. It will be the foundation of a way of life which will enable us to live in the "house of the Lord forever."

Yesterday you were asked to reread Chapters Seven and Eight in preparation for today's activities. These chapters outlined the practice of the presence of God. This day will be committed to this way of life. Your "work" for today is to practice the Presence as outlined in the chapters.

Day Thirty-One

A perfect prayer . . .

Prayer takes many forms. There is a story told of a westerner who visited Mother Teresa of Calcutta. As they were talking, a young nun came to the Mother and said she had been with the Christ all day long. The visitor was surprised because he thought the sisters were with the beggars and people dying in the streets of the city. Mother Teresa said he was correct but the beggar the young sister spoke of was the Christ in one of his disguises.

The actions of the young nun were the perfect prayer. They resulted in a vision that could see the Christ where others might see a beggar.

Recall an event in Jesus' life which was a perfect prayer. Either describe the event or indicate the scripture.

Day Thirty-Two

In service to others . . .

Praying for others is the work of the person who is one with God. In first century Christianity there were numerous healings, and they have continued through the ages, but it seems healings and expressions of divine power are not as prevalent as they used to be. God is as willing as always. The need is as great as it has ever been, but we have lost an awareness of the principles through which the power of God is expressed.

We have lost our focus. In Jesus' ministry attention was given to God, not the people with the needs. For too long we have tried to repair and fix the human condition rather than open ourselves to the revelation of our wholeness and completeness in Spirit. With Jesus' human eyes, He saw the need, but His purpose was not maintenance. He knew the first need was not that of the person whose body was sick, but for the "healer" to give his or her attention to God. Once Spirit reveals itself to us, we will see nothing to heal, for our "vision" will be heavenly. This consciousness then manifests the perfection which is natural to Spirit.

Perhaps you know someone in need, and you want to pray for him or her. Follow these guidelines and allow Spirit to reveal itself to you.

1. Your work is not to do maintenance on the person in need.

2. Nor is God's work maintenance. God's work is creativity.

3. Take your attention away from the person, and give the gift of your attention to Spirit.

4. The issue is whether you will make yourself available to Spirit.

5. Because of these insights, do not use "you statements" like "you are whole and well." At this time, the issue is not physical healing. It is spiritual awareness—yours, not the person for whom you are praying. Instead use I statements like the ones that follow:

Spirit and I are one.
In me there is no sickness.
I am an expression of pure life.
Whole and complete am I.
It matters not the condition of the body.
The body does not change what Spirit has made.
Resting in silent repose is Life,
ready to well up as me—who I truly am.
I let the revelation come.

Day Thirty-Three

A consciousness of God is the "healer."

As you practice the principles of healing as outlined in Chapter Nine and in Day Thirty-Two, an avenue is opened which allows Spirit's expression. We of ourselves can do nothing, but we do have our work to do. It is to give our attention to Spirit and to allow the revelation to come. In the instant there is no need, only God, the healing springs forth mightily.

The process is simple. We ascend to the High Meadow where we wait for the Silence. We speak the highest truth we know. We use "I" statements and think or affirm words we would speak if we were spiritual beings. There is no need in these words, only truth. And Spirit has a channel through which to make itself known upon the earth.

It is clear. God is the healer. Actually, it is more accurate and more in tune with our approach to life to say, a consciousness of God is the healer.

Today ponder these things in your heart and know you can be a servant of God.

Day Thirty-Four

Today I am willing to enter the Quiet.

Declaring, *Today I am willing to enter the Quiet,* does not insure I will experience the calm, peace, and renewal of the Quiet, but it is a beginning. It is good to be aware of the mansions one will enter when prayer is a part of one's life. The Quiet is one of the special gifts we receive when we enter the kingdom of God.

When we are upset, ill, or unsure of ourselves, the Quiet is God's assurance we are not alone. Remember, before a seeker can enter the Quiet, he or she first "climbs" to the High Meadow and waits.

May the following ideas be helpful in making you available to Spirit. As you abide with the ideas, you "climb" to the High Meadow. While in this elevated, feel good state of human consciousness, there is much waiting. After a time, Grace comes and shows you the way to the Quiet.

I am a willing soul.
I bring only my desire for God to this meeting place.
As a human being I have my human needs, but they have no place here.
This is a sacred place where there are no needs.
Willingness I bring.
Trust is my gift.
Knowing that all is well.
I am God's. What am I to fear?
So I am willing. I am trusting.
And to these two I add listening.
It is not sound I listen for.

It is more than listening.
I am sensitive to the Presence.
I am willing, trusting, listening.
And now there is waiting.
Just waiting . . . expectantly . . .
And when the mind drifts down the valley
away from the High Meadow, I become willing
again . . . trusting again.
I listen again . . . and I wait . . . again . . .

Day Thirty-Five

Today I am willing to enter the Blessed State.

When we have a task before us, it is the Blessed State that will see us through. It comes after contact with Spirit and releases the creativity and wisdom of God into our life and into the world. Writers, poets, artists, homemakers, teachers, and athletes can all experience the Blessed State. Often we enter this mansion without a conscious effort toward God, but nevertheless the need for a high state of human consciousness and letting go are prerequisites to entering the Blessed State.

As you are aware, declaring *Today I am willing to enter the Blessed State,* does not make it happen. In fact, we cannot make anything happen when it comes to a spiritual life. However, the Blessed State will be a constant companion when we dedicate ourselves to a closer walk with God. Figuratively speaking, Spirit is always looking for an avenue of expression. Each human being is a potential door through which the power and presence of God are made manifest, but only those who are turned Godward are true candidates to become servants of God.

May the following ideas be helpful in making you available to Spirit. As you abide with the ideas, you "climb" to the High Meadow. While in this elevated, feel good state of human consciousness, there is much waiting. After a time, Grace comes and shows you the way to the Blessed State. Think of yourself as having a task before you. It could be associated with work or perhaps you are open to new ideas so you can solve some problem. Then rest quietly and know . . .

I of myself can do nothing.
It is not I but the Presence which does the work.
I am willing to be an open door through which Spirit enters
and is a blessing.
My work is to be still, to climb to the High Meadow
And to wait . . .
There is an answer.
It is always a consciousness of God.
From this center all true circles are drawn.
I am willing for the mind of God to be active in me.
May any barriers to God's expression be
cleansed.
The door is swung wide.
The path is clear.
Wisdom and creativity are flowing like a river.
Like a parched land, I am nourished.
I thirst no more.
I know what to do.
I am watching God at work.
Thankful. In awe . . . humble.
I am blessed to be a blessing.
And now all that remains is waiting . . .
And Grace comes and takes me to the Blessed State.
And then there is action . . . work.
Sacred work, the work of God.

Day Thirty-Six

In the Silence.

Day Thirty-Six is a reminder of the powerful principle of the Silence. It is the central mansion, the fountainhead of all good. Silence is usually a brief state in which we are not aware of thought, feeling, image, or messages from our five senses. God is beyond all sensation and human faculties. Our five senses allow us to experience the world of manifestation; and our human faculties of thought, feeling, and imagination are designed to be avenues for Spirit's expression on earth. Our five senses and human faculties cannot record Spirit. They were never designed for this purpose.

And yet Spirit is, and for a brief moment, we can experience the Presence. How will we know we have been in the Silence? Our lives will change. The Quiet may follow our entry into the Silence or maybe the Blessed State. Today give yourself without reservation to Spirit. The Silence awaits you.

Day Thirty-Seven

I drink from the limitless reservoir of the Presence.

Each of us wants to live life in peace and with the understanding all things are working together for good. When challenging situations arise in our lives, and inevitably they do, we want to respond rather than react to people and conditions. This is destined to be our way of life, but we will not live life this way unless we have built up a reservoir of spiritual consciousness from which we can drink when the stresses of life confront us.

Every day of our lives we turn the water faucet fully expecting water to flow to meet our needs. This is made possible because of a reservoir which we cannot see. Ideally, water flows into the reservoir each day at a rate greater than the demands of the community it serves. If the reservoir is empty, when we open the faucet, there will be no water.

It is for this reason daily prayer and meditation are so necessary. Through daily prayer and meditation, a spiritual reservoir is built up in us which we can draw upon when needed. This is our responsibility. How spiritual consciousness manifests itself is the business of Spirit.

How will you build up your spiritual reservoir today? Was there a time in the past when you turned to God or to the spiritual reservoir and it was empty? If the answer is yes, why was this so?

Day Thirty-Eight

Prayer simplifies my life.

Prayer has simplified our life. We used to be filled with many desires and each one seemed paramount. It had to be fulfilled. The quietness of prayer has revealed to us that the fulfillment of one desire will bring us all that is necessary. Now God consciousness enlivens us. Things and activities which take away from this awareness have passed away. Life is simplified.

We used to want many things, but now our greatest "possession" is an awareness of Spirit. This is the coin of the realm which provides for each earthly need. Actually, the earthly needs are not what they used to be, for we know as spiritual beings we have all we need.

Has your life been simplified because of prayer? Have you acted upon impulses and urges which promised life anew? For instance, have you wanted to spend more time alone? Have you wanted to read spiritual literature or change your eating habits?

When we turn our attention Godward, ideas and proposed changes rise from within us. They are to be examined and in many cases heeded, for they are divine guidance.

What is your next step in simplifying your life?

Day Thirty-Nine

Prayer brings purpose to my life.

Anyone who has prayed has prayed the prayer, "Not my will, but Yours be done." When we are willing to act upon inner guidance, purpose begins to rise from within us. Usually at first, we are given some simple or seemingly mundane task to perform. If we are willing and obediently follow this inner urge, more tasks lie ahead.

Obviously, when we are willing to do the Father's will, we have purpose. Spirit is always "looking" for someone to be an avenue for all that Spirit is. As your prayer life unfolds, your purpose will become evident. With it will come all the resources necessary to do what must be done by you. It will take time, but with persistence and an allegiance to knowing God, you will know what to do!

Do you have a sense of purpose now? If you do, write what it is.

If you are not sensing your purpose, what must you do to allow Spirit its avenue into the world?

Day Forty

I am a thread in the hem of the garment.

Prayer appears to be a lonely business. We go into our closet and shut the door. We go alone to the mountain or the desert, and let Spirit reveal itself to us. The closer walk with God begins with the individual and his or her desire to know God. They (person and desire) go alone and find that alone means with God.

This practice has been happening for thousands of years, but it is only the beginning. Time and time again they who have encountered the Almighty are quickened to action. Illumination occurs in the mountain or desert, but then they return to the valley, to the villages, and cities of the land. They are servants of God and, although they return again and again to the Silence, Spirit always directs them to serve in the world.

Some people become well known. Others work as gardeners, mothers, teachers, and executives. They are known only to those who work with them. They are the voice, hands, feet, and eyes of Spirit. Simple people living simple lives of service.

Do you remember the story in Jesus' ministry when the woman who had been bleeding for twelve years touched the hem of His garment? She touched not only cloth, but the consciousness of God. We can be threads in the hem of the garment, always extended to humanity as a help in every need. A closer walk with God ultimately makes this our work.

It is now your work. It will be necessary for you to climb to the High Meadow and wait. From these two acts, your closer walk will unfold. It will be a life beyond your human dreams. Are you willing?

How To Form a
"Closer Walk With God"
Prayer Group

It is good to come apart awhile and give ourselves to God. Each true seeker must do this, but it is also fruitful to pray with others. Closer Walk With God Prayer Groups are called Gatherings and are based on Jesus' statement, *"For where two or three are gathered in my name, there am I in the midst of them"* (Matthew 18:20). A Gathering consists of at least two people who have made knowing God the central issue in their lives.

Do not let this "group" be an attempt to have your human needs fulfilled. The closer walk with God is about God, not earthly needs. Jesus issued a challenge to humankind two thousand years ago. *"Seek first his kingdom . . . and all these things shall be yours as well"* (Matthew 6:33). When we pray the prayer of the spiritual being, we put aside our human needs and acknowledge God is what we want. When this desire is met, all things are added unto us. Jesus' statement is not only a challenge; it is a promise, and those who pray the prayer of the spiritual being know it is true!

Consider carefully who you want your prayer partner(s) to be. Gatherings take weekly commitment which stretches into years. Because of your collective dedication, your spiritual lives will deepen as you explore the kingdom of God. When you know who your prayer partner(s) are, write down their name(s).

151

No one can dictate a Gathering's journey and what will happen as you commit yourselves to the prayer of the spiritual being, but it is helpful to have a road map when you travel. Gatherings usually follow nine steps which help the spiritual friends become increasingly aware of their spiritual nature.

Getting Started

First there must be spiritual friends who are willing to gather weekly for prayer, meditation, and waiting. A time and a place are agreed upon. Each week a leader is chosen to lead the Gathering through the nine steps and to introduce the weekly meditation theme.

At first it is good for Gatherings to utilize various meditative techniques, but please remember the heart of prayer is waiting. Usually, Gatherings become focused and are lifted up through the spoken word. We use Paul's method of thinking about that which is lovely, pure, and just. The leader guides the spiritual friends through steps 1-6. In step seven the meditative theme for the Gathering is introduced. Usually the leader will guide the spiritual friends into a relaxed state perhaps by asking the seekers to breathe deeply or become aware of their breathing. Or maybe, the leader will use first person and speak words of peace and serenity to the various parts of the body. Next there is a brief time of waiting (2-3 minutes). Then the meditation begins.

The Steps

Each person affirms out loud the first five steps of the Gathering. For instance, Mary may say out loud, "I release my human need to find a new job." (If there is no specific human need in Mary's life currently, she might say, "I release my human needs.") Then the next person would enter into the first step and so forth until all have shared step one. Then the group moves to step two.

1. **I release my human need** . . . (express the specific human need, if there is one).

This is an ideal beginning for a Closer Walk With God Gathering, because the purpose of prayer is to know God and what it means to be made in God's image and likeness rather than to have our human needs fulfilled. However, our needs will be met as we put God first. Gatherings are essentially spiritual friends accepting Jesus' challenge to seek first the kingdom. "But seek first his kingdom . . . and all these things shall be yours as well" (Matthew 6:33).

2. **I accept my human condition so I can accept my spiritual nature.** Each individual speaks the statement.

Gatherings do not ignore human needs. They assign them their proper place in our lives. Much of humanity's actions are an attempt to change the outer world. This is not our way. The first step in a transformed life or world is acceptance. Unless we accept our humanity, we will not be able to express our divinity. Therefore, we do not ignore our problems, we accept them, not as a permanent part of our lives, but as a part of the journey. The important thing is we do not try to change the outer condition. Our purpose is knowing God. We cannot serve God and change our earthly experience at the same time. God first, then the world.

3. I willingly release any part of my human self which is a barrier to God. Each individual speaks the statement.

There are parts of us which stand as a barrier to Spirit's work. We may or may not be conscious of them, but they are there. You see, Spirit does not force revelation and spiritual awakening upon us. There must be willingness on our part. However, the forces of the universe are always prepared to express themselves in and through us.

4. I willingly forgive others. Each individual speaks the statement.

5. I willingly forgive myself. I am precious to God. Each individual speaks the statement.

The primary blockage to spiritual awareness is unforgiveness of others and ourselves. Following Jesus' example we call this "leaving our gift at the altar." *"So if you are offering your gift at the altar, and there remember that your brother has something against you, leave your gift there before the altar and go; first be reconciled to your brother, and then come and offer your gift"* (Matthew 5:23-24). During a Gathering, steps four and five are an acknowledgment of this important part of spiritual growth. There are suggestions in the forty day guide on how to "be reconciled to your brother" that can help you experience forgiveness. And, of course, there will be meditative experiences in the Gathering which will allow you to discover how precious you and your "brother" are to God.

6. I acknowledge that a consciousness of God is the answer . . . that LIFE is a consciousness of God.

Step six is taken as a group affirmation and serves to lead the Gathering into its time of meditation, prayer, and Silence. This statement is the heart of the closer walk with God. We are destined to become aware of our Creator. This is life. It is not enough to believe God is the answer. This speaks of God's potential to lift us up and help us through the valleys. Only when we awaken is the power and presence of God allowed to begin its reign of peace, love, and joy.

7. Introduction of meditative theme for the day.

It is best if each Gathering has a leader who is responsible for introducing the weekly theme for meditation and prayer. It is not necessary for everyone to lead the sharing time, particularly for those whose humanity is shy and retiring, but it is encouraged that eventually each participant lead the Gathering on a regular, rotating basis.

Careful attention should be given to gently lead your spiritual friends into and out of meditation, prayer, and the Silence. Music can be used as a background if this is preferred, but, also, experiment with times when there is earthly silence. The Gathering leader has the responsibility of guiding the spiritual friends to the High Meadow. Usually, this is accomplished by the spoken word—using affirmation and denial in first person. These statements of truth should be those a spiritual being would speak. Examples are given in the forty day guide.

It is recommended the meditative/prayer portion of the Gathering be about forty minutes. During this time, there should be numerous two to three minute periods of silence and near the end of the forty minutes, there should be a longer period of silence . . . perhaps fifteen minutes. The brief periods of silence allow the mind to begin to wander. The words spoken after the two to three minutes serve to refocus the mind upon God. This process is repeated again and again.

Finally, the silence becomes extended to allow Grace to come and take us from the High Meadow into the Quiet, the Blessed State, or the Silence.

8. I have learned in whatever state I am to be content. Knowing God is enough.

The leader is to gently bring the spiritual friends back to an awareness of the physical world by drawing attention to sounds, and breath, and the body. The meditation and prayer time concludes with the group declaring, "I have learned in whatever state I am to be content. Knowing God is enough."

9. As everyone becomes conscious once again of his or her surrounding, the leader stresses three things.

(1). There is to be no discussion of what happened in our interior world during the prayer/meditation time.

(2). We are not to grade ourselves as to how well we are doing in our prayer life. "All is well" is a phrase we like to use.

(3). We have gathered in God's name. This is what is important. We will gather again.

Conclusion

When my mother gave birth to me, it was more her birthday than mine. I drew my first breath, but I am not sure when I came alive. It had nothing to do with breathing air. Perhaps it was when I was a child and sat alone at the side of the sea. Regardless of when it was, it was Silence which first gave birth to me. It was Silence that brought me to life.

I have died and been born many times since that day. I was conscious of my Creator, so I was alive, and then my world and its woes seemed more important than God, and I fell asleep again. This process has not ceased. I am born again, and then I die. But each time I am born anew, I am more aware of life's source—a consciousness of God.

This is why *A Closer Walk With God* was written, to help others come alive. Not to breathe air, but to realize one can perpetually breathe the breath of the Almighty. I have had only a few wants in writing this book. My hope is that eventually everyone will give himself or herself to Spirit in his or her own unique way. I know there are many different roads to God just as there are many different techniques of prayer. However, I trust *A Closer Walk With God* has explored some of the ground which is common regardless of the technique used.

As you continue your quest of the Infinite, please know you are not alone. People around the world are united with you. Look around you, and you will discover people everywhere who are enjoying and challenged by the closer walk with God.

AUDIO CASSETTES BY JIM ROSEMERGY

RETREAT TAPES
LIVING THE MYSTICAL LIFE TODAY MEDITATIONS
INTO THE SILENCE MEDITATIONS
A CLOSER WALK WITH GOD

FOR FURTHER INFORMATION
CONTACT
JIM ROSEMERGY AT:

INNER JOURNEY
RR 1; BOX 1966
SUNRISE BEACH, MO 65079